Papercuts and Glitter Jars

An adoption and life journey

Written By: Tracy M. Dayment

DAYMENT
LEGACY BOOKS

ISBN: 979-8-9900768-0-8

For my daughter Diana Aurora. My life wouldn't be as chaotic without you, but I wouldn't change it for the world.

Table of Contents

Preface

It's funny the way life works sometimes. It's said that everything happens for a reason. It's hard to believe when times are tough, but days, months, or sometimes even years later the view may be crystal clear. I have a husband, a daughter, a couple of dogs, a house, a good career, and a dream of becoming an author. None of that felt like it would happen and none of it was easy, but I kept chugging along living the best life I could. New people, new experiences, and new adventures are always around the corner. Sometimes you don't even have to look for them, other times it may feel like a fight to get there.

This is a true story about how my life has become what it is over the last twenty plus years. Meeting my husband, deciding on adoption, and raising a child with special needs. I don't write this to be an inspiration, I write this to show even through the challenges, everything is possible. Looking back at the last twenty years, I still don't know how I did it, how I survived heartbreak, how I survived the adoption journey, and how I am surviving this thing called life. I'm happy to announce that I'm still happily chugging along.

Chapter One

My life into true adulthood started in the year 2000. I was twenty years old and working full-time as a business travel administrator. Just like the travel agents, I was able to take advantage of travel perks. At one point I saw a fax come into the office. With a certain airline I could get up to two plane tickets for only $35 each. I was ecstatic. Still living with my mom at the time, I rushed home to tell her. I wanted so badly to go to Las Vegas with her just after my twenty-first birthday. I was the oldest of my friends, so I had to go with someone older than me to be able to fully celebrate. She gave me the news that she had a work conference during the long weekend I wanted to go. Looking back, I don't know why I just didn't change to a different weekend, but here's an example of everything happens for a reason. Instead, I took it as an absolute no and called my best friend at the time and made plans to go elsewhere.

The year before, in 1999, I worked in Orlando, Florida at Walt Disney World's Magic Kingdom for a college program. I met a friend, Doug, who lived in Pennsylvania and thought it would be fun to go visit him. My friend, Kirsten, and I packed our bags and headed to Philadelphia International Airport. We didn't have any big plans ahead of us, just to escape, see his college campus, and have a good time. The flight was uneventful as you hope all flights are and we called Doug to let him know to come pick us up. When we first saw Doug, he had someone else with him. It turned out to be his college roommate, Tim. The four of us had a fun drive over to our hotel for the next couple of nights.

Doug pretty much ditched Kirsten and I as he had a girlfriend to attend to and Tim kept us both company. He even called into work so we wouldn't have to be alone. Fast forward through the next two days, Tim and I started to feel a connection. We really enjoyed each other's company, had a similar sense of humor, and of course the attraction was there. The last night was September 17th, and it was very late at night. We took a walk around outside and stumbled upon a gazebo at the hotel. We stayed in that gazebo for hours talking. Tim pulled out a piece of paper from his back pocket and asked if he could read it to me. It was a poem. A poem that he wrote earlier in the day. A poem he wrote just for me. A poem that he asked if we could start dating. I was blown away. No one has ever done that for me. It was so sweet and romantic, and I obviously said yes.

The next morning was the flight back home, to Chicago, about eight hundred miles away. I just met this fantastic guy and now we already had to say our goodbyes. I was devastated. I knew getting into this we would have to have a long-distance relationship but had no idea what that would actually look like. I barely had many relationships before this, how would this possibly work.

Plus, we were only together for about three days. Would that connection be so strong that we could keep it going?

The next several months we talked via computer and prepaid calling cards. Calling through the computer was tough. I'm grateful there was that option at the time, but it was dial up internet. Basically, you logged into the internet and pulled up a program that you can dial and call. The microphone was large and had to make sure you talked directly into it. There were many times it was tough to hear the person on the other line, other times it worked great. However, if anyone in your house picked up the phone, or even just randomly, the computer would disconnect hearing those dreadful goodbyes of the internet. It was frustrating. This is where the calling cards came in. We would each buy $20 of calling cards at a time, taking turns being the one that called. We would talk for hours (or for however many minutes the calling cards allowed us). Just about every day we would talk. We both were in college and had jobs, so we had to work around each other's schedules, but somehow it just worked for us.

I couldn't handle being apart for so long, so after a month, I booked another flight to Philadelphia. No crazy cheap deal this time. We spent the entire weekend together. Watching football, talking, just hanging out together. It was almost magical. The weekend soon came to an end and again had to say our goodbyes. He would walk me through the airport terminal and right to the gate and would sit with me until I had to board the plane. He stayed until the plane backed away. I could see him from my window seat. I was holding back my tears as we had to do this long-term relationship thing again. Back to the internet calling and prepaid cards. I couldn't even guess how much we spent on those cards.

In November, Tim decided it was his turn to come out to me. He booked a train to take him from Philadelphia to Chicago at Christmas time during school break. We were able to spend an entire week together! We had been dating for three months by this point and this was going to be the longest we had been together physically. It was amazing. I had the opportunity to show him around town, meet some of my friends, and he could meet my parents. It was a big trip. The week went so fast before I knew it, I was taking him back to the train station for his long journey home. Every time we said goodbye made it even harder.

We both were now in our last semester of college. We both had to concentrate on our studies if we wanted to graduate. Graduating meant we may just be able to end the long distance. We went through the entire beginning of the year until May that we saw each other again. I flew out for his graduation and party and was able to meet his entire family and friends. It was a great few days, but again, I needed to get back because I still had another month of schooling. In June he flew out to me to celebrate. We did it! We finally were college graduates! It didn't take long for our future to truly begin. In August of 2001 he moved to the suburbs of Chicago to be with me, and we had our very first apartment together. No more long distance for us. We made it through that year!

The infamous September 11th happened while we were living together for only a few weeks. I worked in high rises, and he was concerned. He worked night shifts, and I didn't even see him until very late at night. That day took a toll on everyone. We mourned the loss of all those people, we mourned the loss of our great nation, we mourned as a country for a very long time. On September 17th, exactly one year after we started to date, we spent the night enjoying each other's company. He didn't know how to cook, so he made some delicious sandwiches for the both of us. We then went for a drive to a nearby gazebo, similar to the one where he read me the poem. After some talking, hugging, and slow dancing to the music in our heads, he pulled out a ring from his pocket and popped the question. Here we were, becoming engaged. I couldn't believe it. Just before I met Tim, I was doubting I would ever meet the one and now we are engaged. Upon spreading the news, we had so many comments about how that happy news was greatly needed in the time of sadness. It was a tough decision for him to pull out the ring during such a great period of mourning. He decided to keep to his plan, as the seventeenth of September was incredibly special to us. We told everyone we could, and I was actually thanked by some coworkers for giving some much-needed happy news.

Over the next two years, we planned the wedding. In our little one-bedroom apartment we would do crafts and make wedding programs. We would do bridal expos and cake tastings. Never losing sight that our love wasn't just about this one day. Yes, we wanted a day that we would remember forever, one that our guests would think back to and smile, but we were most excited to make our love official and be Mr. and Mrs. for the rest of our lives.

Throughout planning an entire wedding, we were also planning a huge change in our lives. We had the opportunity to move to Arizona and after a great deal of talking, we decided to go for it. It was a change we both felt we needed. He didn't have any family or friends in Illinois, and I always wanted to leave the state. If we were going to do it, this was the right time. Two months after we were married, in August of 2003, we packed up the truck and headed out west. New beginnings all around.

The adjustment period for me was a bit hard. Trying to find a job that I really wanted to do was tough. I finally settled in, and it soon began to feel at home. In November that year, we went looking for new homes and purchased our first home together. It was really a dream come true. Everything was falling into place. We talked about having kids and wanted to in the near future but wanted to get Arizona under our belt first. After about a year, the time came. We were ready to settle down and start a family of our own. We had one dog Hunter already and were ready to add a human child to the mix. What we didn't know is how much of a challenge that would be. People have babies all the time. How is it that we try and try and month after month we end up in disappointment? This couldn't be happening. My own sister had kids every other year. It was devastating. Every month I went through a period of depression yet trying to put on a happy face for everyone around us. I cried myself to sleep countless nights.

When someone goes through infertility, as much as you try to be there for them, you just can't relate. I had a work friend who was going through it at the same time. However, our situations were different from each other. No two situations will ever be the same. I wanted two kids, probably boys, and we would live our fantasy life happily ever after. It takes a lot to realize the dream bubble doesn't have to pop, it just needs to be shifted and that was still a hard pill to swallow.

After we started healing from the doctors' words of not having kids the typical way, we did a lot of research. There were options we never thought we would have to consider. Options that cost a lot of money. We were a young couple in our twenties with mediocre jobs which were enough to just pay the bills. Yes, we would have some extra money to support a baby, but there was no way we would be able to spend tens of thousands of dollars on procedures that may not have any positive results, or would need to be repeated if the first procedure didn't work. It was a tough decision what to do. We were very fortunate that our relationship with each other was so strong that we were able to fight through this and come out the other side. I understand couples that aren't able to get through it. It wasn't easy. At least one, if not both, of the individuals feels they are to blame or are the broken ones. It was definitely a challenging few years. Here comes that saying again. Everything happens for a reason. In these few years, we didn't see it this way, we just saw ourselves failing to make a family of our own. Looking back after everything we've gone through; I can finally see it crystal clear.

Chapter Two

Choosing adoption was not an easy decision to come by. It's hard to shift dreams thinking your whole life you would be a mom by carrying a baby yourself. I never thought I would be one to adopt. I never thought I would be strong enough to go through that process. I don't want to make it seem like adoption is just a secondary thought. Adoption is a beautiful thing and to many it is the only way to go, but for me I just didn't give it much thought in my early years.

After many tears and sleepless nights, we decided to go for it. It must be the path we were meant to take. We always watch television specials about kids that need a home for Christmas. Those tearjerker shows that make you think you need to save the world. It hit us hard one year. We called the number to start working through the foster care system. We don't live in the biggest county in our state, but just next to it. The person on the line didn't have any information for our county so we were not able to get any information. We obtained another phone number that we reached out to. We never received any call backs after a few messages were left. On the website it showed meeting dates for orientation that we would need to attend. Getting excited, we were headed to our very first meeting. Everywhere we go, we arrive early. No one was there. After about ten minutes two other couples showed up. It was starting to feel real. As six o'clock was hitting, there were no representatives getting prepped. Six fifteen and still no representatives. Six thirty and no one in sight. Our hearts sank. We were so excited to attend this informational meeting and so sad no one showed up. We decided to leave, along with the other couples who were there. We assumed something must have come up that whoever was going to give the talk just couldn't make it. It's fine, we'll just catch a meeting on another day.

About a month later, there was another meeting. This one about a half hour the other direction from the first. It was on a Saturday rather than a weekday, so we were in absolutely no rush. We could enjoy our whole day and get all the information they would give us. We showed up early as usual. No other couple showed up this time, it was just us. Eight o'clock came and went and there were no representatives. We just stood outside feeling defeated. Are we not supposed to adopt? Are we not supposed to go through the foster care system? We've heard some tough stories about fostering to adopt but were ready to take it on. We have just gone through two no show appointments. If it is this hard to get started, I can't even imagine how it will be once we are in the middle of the process. We just had to take it as a sign and to stop trying this route.

We let a few years go by, enjoying life to the fullest. There was still that emptiness in our hearts. Our family was not complete. Our child was still out there somewhere. It was up to us to figure out how to do it. We went on an Alaskan cruise, just Tim and I. Alaska was one of the most beautiful places I've ever seen. I felt my head was cleared out by the fresh air and smells. I felt at peace. I felt stronger. I felt like I was ready to handle more. The moment we got home, I started to research. The internet became my best friend. How can we adopt? There must be other ways. We looked at several agencies and I just couldn't figure out how we would be able to afford it. I looked at other future adoption family's profiles. How would we ever compete. Who would ever see our profile and decide we were the right ones for their baby. It seemed like an impossible process.

Back to the drawing board. I just couldn't justify the costs. At the time, in 2012, it was over sixty thousand dollars just to go through the process. If delays came up or a snag in the process happened, it would cost more. What wasn't included in that cost was the birth mother's doctor bills, the cost for flights back and forth assuming the birth mother lived far, the cost of hotels, food, etc. At this point, we're talking close to a hundred thousand dollars and there's still the possibility that the birth mother could still change her mind at any time. I'm all for the ability that the birth mother can change her mind. It's her son or daughter and she may have found a support system she didn't know she had. I just don't know if I could handle the rejection after getting my hopes up so high. I already had a good-sized mortgage; would the bank even give me a loan that high. My biggest upset by this was if I was spending that much money on the adoption, how would I ever have enough money to raise the child. I didn't think that would be fair to the child. I'm supposed to be giving them the best life possible, but I wouldn't be able to do that with that much added debt.

Something I didn't think in the past I would consider was an international adoption. I was in the mindset that there were so many kids in the United States that needed loving homes, why would I go out of the country? I changed my mind when I realized how hard and expensive adoption was in my own country. How my country made it so hard for these children to find homes they deserve. Even sitting here today, it hurts my heart to know there's so many children needing homes and so many adults with homes to open to these children, yet so many messy hurdles to jump through. It makes it nearly impossible for the average middle class couple.

I started to go down the international adoption route to see what I could discover. There were several countries that allowed Americans to adopt. They all had different rules, different timelines, and different costs associated with them. I almost went the route of going through Russia and am thankful I avoided that as within the year they no longer were allowing Americans to adopt. So many devastating stories of families in the middle or at the end of an adoption and had to leave their child behind. I then found Ukraine. I didn't know a whole lot about

Ukraine at the time, just that it was near Russia. I found the whole process to be interesting. Do not take this information to heart as I'm sure it has changed, if even allowed, at this time. All my information is just my own experience in 2012.

Ukraine looked to be a beautiful country. They speak a combination of Russian and Ukrainian. I read others' adoption blogs, watched several vlogs, and read on the history of Ukraine. I found several success stories. More good stories over bad. Some people even spelled out the whole process. I finally felt like this was our path. This is the way we were meant to adopt. Our child could very well be in that country already. For the first time in years, I felt hope. I felt excited. I was ready to get this process started and find my inner strength that I didn't know existed.

Chapter Three

Ukraine was now my pursuit. What made me decide on Ukraine? The main reason was we didn't need to hire a lawyer, we were able to do it all ourselves. This made a considerable difference in cost. Not only the cost difference, but I prefer not to trust other middleman people. I would rather do it myself. I feel more in control that way, even if the whole process seems daunting. Tim agreed with my findings and after several long talks, we decided this was going to be the path we were going to walk. In July of 2012 we officially were on our way to build our family.

As excited as we were, we were also so incredibly stressed and scared. This would be the true test to see how strong we are. Adoption is definitely not for the faint of heart. The first thing we had to do was to look at their restrictions. We had to be at least twenty-one years old, married, and have a minimum income. We passed the first test. In Ukraine if you are from another country, you are not allowed to adopt a child younger than five years old unless they are part of a sibling group. For example, you can adopt a three-year-old if you are adopting their older sibling who is five or older. We were okay with this as we were getting older and felt the older children get overlooked more often anyways. At least we would get to miss out on the dirty diaper stages! The only other way we could adopt a child younger than five would be if the child was severely disabled. While I would love to save the world and adopt anyone, I knew in my heart my husband and I would not be able to handle that type of need.

After becoming invested in going through Ukraine, the adoption process was about to begin. In our own county we had to find a place to have our fingerprints taken. We also had to apply for USCIS or Form I-600A. In addition to that, we had to have a home study done, then turn in all that paperwork to the local courthouse.

Having a home study done can be very intimidating. It's hard to invite a stranger into your house to completely judge the way you live. You tend to question everything that you have in your house, or will your pets behave themselves when the home study conductor is there. It really was scarier in my head than it turned out to be. First things first, we had to find an accredited agency and schedule an appointment for a meeting at their office. It was nice to meet her beforehand as we did feel a little more comfortable later. At the office visit she asked us many questions. Why we wanted to adopt, where we were going to adopt, our income, pretty much opening our entire life to this lady. It's one of the hardest things about adoption. There is no privacy when trying to become approved. After the office visit we scheduled a time for her to come to the house.

We cleaned until everything was spotless. We made sure the yard was picked up from our dogs. We were so nervous. This was the lady that would allow or deny us the possibility to adopt. She looked to make sure the smoke detectors were in working order, we had a fire extinguisher in the kitchen, we had a bedroom for the future kid. Turns out, the home study wasn't as scary as we were making it out to be. She didn't care if the house was spotless, she didn't care if the dogs were hyper, as long as they weren't aggressive. She went back to her office and filled out all our approved paperwork! It was such a relief. After we took all our papers to the courthouse, we just had to sit and wait for the court's decision to come back. There was no court date, no in person interview, they were just reviewing our paperwork to make a determination if we were good enough to have children. After several weeks, we got our letter. We were finally approved and ready to go!

Once approved, we moved to our next step. We had tons of paperwork to fill out. It really is amazing how much you had to prove yourself to adopt when anyone having a child naturally can have one. I do feel though this has made me a better mom. Having to prove myself repeatedly really made me want to show the world that I could do it. All the forms that we needed to fill out were listed on a website. We followed a few blogs at the time so that confirmed what we needed. After printing all the papers, it was time to get our writer's cramp going. Wow, that was painful. Papercuts, writer's cramp, eyes glazing over, it truly was a struggle. These were forms like letters of proof of employment our employers had to write up and copies of our latest medical records. It took several weeks to obtain everything we needed. Once everything was filled out completely, we had to bundle it all up and take it to our bank to get notarized. Even the banker was surprised how many documents we needed to have notarized. It took a while. Once we had all the documents in order and all notarized, we had to go to the Secretary of State's office. Here we needed to get all our documents apostilled. An apostille is basically a notary for the notary. They put their embossed stamp on each one of the documents. The seal of approval.

Throughout our research, I did find a lady in Florida that can go through all our paperwork for a fee to make sure it is all in order. This way we wouldn't have to send things back and forth to Ukraine until we got it right. She was well worth the price. We had to make some adjustments, go through the notary and apostille process again and we were complete! In my writing, the whole process doesn't sound too bad, but it did take several months to complete. Our doctors didn't work well with us and wouldn't sign any papers; needless to say, we eventually found a new doctor's office. We needed to obtain a certified marriage license which had to be obtained in person at the courthouse. Thank goodness they allowed my sister to get it for us as it was in Illinois and we lived several states away. There were many bumps in the road, but we managed to keep going.

When going through the Florida lady for help, part of the cost included having a contact in Ukraine. This was especially helpful as we were getting ready to send the package. She would email us and make sure we had everything we needed. We then stopped by the FedEx office and mailed out our three-and-a-half-pound package of paperwork to Ukraine. It was done. Everything we could do here in the states was done. It was up to Ukraine now. That was an exciting time, but also when the stress really began.

We waited for what seemed like years for our approval letter. A letter that would not only show we were approved to adopt, but also give us an appointment date and time that we would need to be in Ukraine. The lady in Ukraine kept making sure we were doing okay in the waiting process. She kept good communication with us. Then there it was. An email that came through. An email stating, we had an appointment on September 10, 2013. I couldn't believe it. I was at work when it came through and I fought with myself whether I should call Tim right away or if I should surprise him when I got home. I couldn't wait. I was way too excited and our airline tickets for Kiev, Ukraine had to be purchased immediately. Our trip was about three weeks away.

We had so much to do in those three weeks that it just flew by. We needed someone to watch over our house and dogs for at least six weeks. I needed to call my human resource department so I could get my FMLA started. We needed to pack, and we needed to take out a whole lot of money from the bank. Packing was an interesting aspect. Living in Arizona, we don't have many cold weather clothes. Living in Ukraine for at least six weeks would mean there would most likely be weather changes going from summer/autumn to early winter. We would be doing laundry while there but didn't want to be wearing the same clothes all the time. We heard things like peanut butter were so expensive that we decided to bring our own, along with snacks we knew we would like. One thing different about a Ukrainian adoption versus other countries is before traveling to the country we don't know who we will be adopting, their age, gender, or even if we would adopt at all. It was taking a big chance. There was always the possibility that this would not work out and we would go home and continue to live our lives as a family of two.

Chapter Four

The biggest question we get is how were we able to afford the adoption? It wasn't easy. We were two lower to middle class people in our twenties. At the same time, I'm very cheap, some may say frugal. I absolutely hate spending money and will be one that buys from a thrift store before I spend full retail price at department stores.

The paperwork fees and the home study we were able to pay for on our own. It was affordable to get the process going. At this point, we didn't really have a plan in place. We were going at it by the skin of our teeth. Not the best way to begin.

We tried some fundraisers that we thought we could pull off. Having no family in the area made it that much harder for us, but not impossible. Having local support would definitely have made things easier with connections or just the extra helping hands.

The first fundraiser was a puzzle. We found a cute puzzle that featured two lions and their little cub. We started selling puzzle pieces to family and friends at five dollars apiece. When they purchased a puzzle piece, their name would go on the back. When the puzzle was complete, we would hang it in our child's room, and it would show her all the people that supported her before she ever came home. We had some success at first. It was a great way for family to help without begging them all for money. It didn't bring in a whole lot of money, but it was a start. At the end we did have a lot of unfilled pieces. I wasn't about to have only half the puzzle filled out. It just felt incomplete. In the end, I filled up the rest of the pieces with names of people that helped us throughout the journey, even if it wasn't in monetary form.

Our second fundraiser was a garage sale. We didn't really have much in our house that we wanted to get rid of, so we had to come up with another plan. Craigslist was popular at the time. I would search for local residents that were having a garage sale. I would reach out to them explaining our story and asking if they would donate all left-over items to us rather than donating them to the thrift store when they were done. We got a lot of positive responses. We ended up moving our vehicles out of the garage and into the driveway to make room for everything. We obtained furniture pieces, clothes, baby items, jewelry, crafts, and the list goes on. On the day of the sale, we brought everything out of the garage into the yard. We made large signs and had a lot of people stop by. We advertised on local sale Facebook sites. We made good money, but I know we could've made more if we did a few things differently.

If we were more organized, I know we would've had more success. We collected so many things on many different weekends. Had I priced everything as we received and placed in item related boxes, I feel it would have been better. There were some weekends we got bombarded with so much stuff it felt out of control, but had I taken the time to sort and price, it would have been worth it.

The other thing would have been to make my signs better. I feel like we could have reached more people by having a more professional sign made at the local office store. It was hard to make signs for everyone to read and know that our sale wasn't like any other sale but was huge.

We should have gone the full weekend, Friday through Sunday. I realized after the fact that so many successful garage sales start on Fridays. Starting that day early would have been great. The other thing is we were so tired that we just packed everything left on Saturday night and donated it. I wish we would have pushed through the exhaustion and continued on Sunday like we originally planned. We went through all the hard work to collect several items we could have tried to sell longer.

Allow early birds and every offer that comes your way. That's something I wish we did. I kept reading online that early birds try to take everything and to be fair not to allow them. That was just dumb on my part. Whether it was sold earlier or later it shouldn't have mattered to me. I had one person interested in a big item and I told them to come back once we opened. Well, guess what. They never came back, and the item never sold. Missed opportunity for sure. The other side of it, yes, we are trying to fund an adoption, which was made clear on the signs, but I should've accepted any offer for the items. We didn't buy any of the things we were selling, we had no emotional tie to them and just wanted them gone for some sort of money. In doing this, we could have made a lot more I'm sure. If someone walked away I would lower the price, but by then, they usually weren't interested anymore. All in all, the sale was a success, but could have been even better.

Our third fundraiser was a little silly. I was making t-shirts with stenciling the word "love" on them written in Ukrainian. There are so many better ways to do stencils now that look more professional, that I would have done if I redid anything. I was cutting stencils out of freezer paper and painting them. Very time consuming. The only people that purchased any of my shirts were our family. However, it was pretty neat because we ended up with pictures of all my closest family wearing their shirts. So, regardless, I love that I did that.

Another big fundraiser I put on was a craft fair. I have been in fairs in the past, but never organized one. I'm a crafty person and gave myself a booth to sell as well. By organizing a fair, I had to find a venue, get permission from the city, and pay the fees. We went to the town next to ours. It was a more convenient location. We found a park that would be affordable and have enough space for about thirty-five different vendors. After everything was approved, we had the summer to find our vendors. I typed up a vendor application and had it submitted to several Facebook sites and newspaper sites to get the word out. I managed to get the word out and had applications coming in. The application fee was thirty-five dollars, and all the money went straight to our adoption. I managed to get about thirty vendors in total. My mom and one of my cousins from California both flew out to help me put this together. It was great to feel the support that I usually didn't feel. They were both a huge help in keeping things organized and helping the vendors with their requests. Things that would have made this better would have been a location closer to a main road. We were at a park, and it was hard to see from the main road. You could tell there was something going on, but it was hard to tell what. I did have signs made, but by the time we hung them up at the big intersections, it looked small. I would have at least had a flip sign made and had someone waving to cars if I were to do it again. There was a waffle breakfast at the Town Hall going on at the same time. My mom and cousin went over there and were bringing people over, that helped tremendously.

All these fundraisers and it was still not even close to enough money that we needed. We looked at different options. Some banks offer adoption loans. Ours, unfortunately, did not. We were looking into some other banks and got a phone call from my mom in the process. She had offered to loan us the remaining amount we needed by cashing in part of her 401k. I couldn't believe she was willing to do that, and I know I am very fortunate that we had that opportunity. I do not like borrowing money from people but was sure to make payment plans to pay her back every single penny we owed her. I made a payment booklet filled with payment coupons, each holding its own due date. I also made a spreadsheet I could fill in after each payment was made. My loan lasted three years and the monthly payment was similar to a car payment. I wouldn't suggest taking money out of a retirement fund, but definitely try to put money aside monthly, similar to a car payment. Over time, it really adds up.

Chapter Five

    The day has finally come. The day we have waited for, for so long. It's travel day! We packed our two suitcases and two backpacks and were ready to head to the airport. After our van picked us up, the skies opened. It was pouring rain the entire drive to the airport. It has been years since we saw rain this bad. Of all days, this is the day mother nature decided we needed to exit a drought. The roads were flooding. The highways were getting backed up and we were getting nervous. After arriving at the airport everything seemed to calm down. We checked in and were ready for our first flight to O'Hare. I loved that we went to this airport. I still had so many family and friends that lived in Chicago that I felt it was their way of cheering us on from only a small distance. We flew to Chicago many times, so we were so used to this flight and luckily nothing of excitement took place.

    On to the next flight! This time we were headed from Chicago O'Hare to Munich, Germany. Our first truly international flight. We went to Grand Cayman once, but that was many years ago on our honeymoon. This flight would take up the majority of the day and the night. We never saw so much seating on a plane before. We were stuck in the middle, since we didn't book our flights early, but it wasn't bad. We got to sit together, watch movies, listen to music, and best of all, they served food. We enjoyed both dinner and breakfast on the same flight. Landing in Germany was beautiful. We only saw it from the air, but I could just tell it was a country I may one day travel back to.

Our final leg was from Munich, Germany to Kiev, Ukraine. At this point we were very done being in airplanes. We were so tired and just wanted a real bed. This flight was only a couple hours, but it felt like forever. And then we landed. We touched down in the country our son or daughter could possibly be. We had to clear customs and then were on our way. After obtaining our luggage, we had to go to the front of the airport to find a person holding a sign with our name on it. We didn't know who this would be, just that he was going to drive us to our temporary apartment. This is when the nervousness and stress really kicked in. We were in a strange country, meeting up with someone we didn't know, getting dropped off to a place we've never been, and any English that was spoken was hard to understand. We had to have so much trust in these people that they were not going to harm us.

We made it to our apartment. He helped us with our luggage in the narrowest elevator I've ever seen and then he left. Inside the apartment was an older lady, Galena, who was waiting for us. There was no time for relaxing, she just jumped on us giving all details for the next day along with a cell phone as ours didn't have an international service. She made me nervous as she told us how much money we needed to pay for the taxi service and started trying to grab all the money I brought with us. Once the language barrier got a little better, I was able to pay him, and she calmed down. Galena advised us in a few hours we would need to go outside behind the Chinese restaurant and meet up with Irina, then she left. Finally, we had time to calm down and relax for a little bit.

The apartment was small, but I really didn't need anything all that big anyways. It had one bedroom, a small bathroom, a small kitchen with a washing machine. I didn't realize dryers were hard to come by over there. It didn't take long to see how spoiled I really was in America. The window opened out with no screens, and I would stick my head outside peering down to the street below. It appeared we were staying in a pretty good area. We did have access to the internet and throughout the trip Tim would still be working. Definitely a perk of a work at home job. We plugged in our international a/c adaptor, then plugged in the computer. Boom! The electricity went out immediately. It was already getting dark, and we didn't know what to do. We were in the apartment for not more than five minutes by ourselves and already blew a fuse. After looking around the apartment we couldn't find a fuse box. We checked in the hallway to see if the lights were on out there, which they were. Confirmed it was us that caused it. We eventually found the fuse box that was actually in the hallway of the apartment rather than in the apartment itself. Finally, we were in business again. Tried plugging things in again, and it was a success.

About two hours later we needed to meet with Irina. She was going to help us throughout the whole adoption process. She spoke better English than Galena, but we still struggled to understand her at times. She explained how the SDA (State Department for Adoptions) appointment would go and made sure we had our phone, passports, and appointment paperwork with us. This was it, one of the days we were waiting for had finally come.

The next morning, we met up with Irina in our business casual attire and walked across Kiev to the SDA. This is the appointment we received the letter about. This is the appointment we will find out which child we would be able to meet. We waited in the hall for our turn to be called. We stood there for only about ten minutes. My stomach was fluttering. I was excited and scared at the same time. A recurring theme throughout the entire process.

Tim and I walked into the room. There were so many binders that filled the wall-to-wall bookshelves. I couldn't believe how many there were. It made me sad to see there were that many children waiting to be adopted. The lady we met with had a binder with her. I often look back and wonder if there was a reason she had that binder or if it was just one she grabbed. Irina was by our side to translate for us. First they looked at our dossier which was part of the paperwork we mailed in. We indicated we wanted just one child. We didn't care if the child was a boy or a girl. Since five was the youngest age we could adopt, we decided to do an age range from five to nine years old. In order to have any chance of adopting a child, we had to indicate we were okay if the child had specific needs, but we said not too severe. She would only show us files that met those criteria.

In the binders, the child's profiles are all printed off with a small write up on each one. Each profile was in its own page protector. She would read a case file and throw it on the little coffee table next to where we were sitting. Irina would then translate, and we would see the child's picture. At first we were really scared. She showed us children that had severe special needs. So severe that they might not live more than a couple more years. At first I didn't know what to do. I know what I'm capable of and what I'm not.

She then carried on. Reading another and another and throwing each one of them down. Then she stopped when she figured we had enough to look through. There was one that caught my attention. It was a little red-headed boy who was five years old. He was adorable. His birthday was actually just two days after mine. What caught my attention was he looked very similar to Tim when he was a young boy.

However, there was one file that kept dropping out of her binder. It would fall, she would put it back in, fall again, put it back in. The last time it would fall, she just decided to leave it on the table. Tim's first pick was this little girl. He had the same reasoning. He picked her because she reminded him of myself when I was younger. At this point we didn't know anything about her since she was just placed on the table without explanation. Her name was Diana. She had dirty blonde hair, brown eyes, and was eight years old. She didn't have any siblings. Her birthday was just two days before Tim's. She had a past heart surgery, and she may have some intellectual delays.

Most of the time, from what I researched, they will say almost every child has intellectual delays who are up for adoption. From what I can tell, it's mostly because they are living their lives in an orphanage and may just get behind. After comparing the two children (which was one of the hardest things to do) we decided to meet Diana.

Chapter Six

Diana was at an orphanage in Vinnytsia, Ukraine. It was about a four- hour drive from Kiev. It was also the job of Irina to call the orphanage and make arrangements for us to visit the next day. In the meantime, we had to change apartments because the owners rented ours out to someone else. Just when we were getting a little bit comfortable we had to be uprooted. We moved and waited for our phone call about meeting Diana.

This apartment smelled funny. There were two bedrooms, one of which Irina would use. It had a kitchen that you had to walk up a step to get to. I tripped over that step repeatedly. There was a tv that we could use. We watch game shows, however not speaking any Ukrainian ourselves, there was only so much we could play along.

The first call came through. They didn't know where she was. We were at a loss. How does the orphanage lose track of her? Irina was in the process of tracking her down. Finally, hours later, we got another call from Irina. Diana was on a summer trip and headed back. We were not exactly sure how long this was going to be. Rather than meeting her the next day, we were going to have to wait a few extra days. The anticipation was killing me. Finally, we got the call that we were good to go and could start heading to Vinnytsia.

It was five in the morning, and we had to meet our driver and Irina in an alleyway just outside of our new apartment. The sun hadn't come up yet and the surrounding area was so quiet. It was raining hard. We were getting an early start to meeting our possible daughter.

The trip was very long. We were still so tired from our flight. I tried to stay awake so I could see where they were taking us. I just couldn't. Every two minutes I would fall back to sleep while leaning on the door. I didn't sleep too well as the anxiety was pushing through me. At one point I woke up and the sky was blue, the grass was green, we were passing by fields, and I saw many sheep. It was the first time I was really able to see Ukraine in its beauty. We drove through small neighborhoods, small farmlands, it was gorgeous. After many more sleeps and awakenings, we finally made it to Vinnytsia. It was pouring down, and the rain was cold. We all ran into a small coffee shop to wait out the storm and for the orphanage to be ready to see us. The taxi driver stayed with us as he would be driving us there. We had some soup to warm up a bit. When the storm lightened up a little, we made a run for it to the toy shop just a few doors down. It is customary to bring a toy for the child we will be visiting. The toy store had the cheapest of toys. Nothing all that neat, just cheap plastic. I found a purple plastic pony I thought she might enjoy. We headed back to the coffee shop to wait some more.

We waited for nearly three hours. It was some of the longest hours, just waiting. Finally, Irina got the call. We were able to go to the orphanage.

The orphanage wasn't all that far away. We entered, and the orphanage had a strong scent of borscht and bread. The director welcomed us in, and we were scooted to a cold, white office. The longest five minutes passed as we anticipated her walking in. Finally, a little eight-year-old girl entered. She appeared to be much smaller than a typical American eight-year-old, I would've thought she was five years old. She had the biggest smile I've ever seen. She waved to us with her whole arm. This was our Diana. I sat on the floor with her and gave her the toy pony. Together we made it gallop and jump. Not sure what else there really is to do with just one pony. She was happy. She was laughing. My heart was melting. I had tears in my eyes. Tears of joy, tears of hope, tears of disbelief. I tried talking with her as best as I could with her not knowing any English and me only knowing a few words of Ukrainian. It didn't matter. We were able to make a connection and enjoy each other's company. We only had about fifteen minutes with her, then off she went. Back to her classroom. While I know we were positive we were going to adopt this little girl, they didn't want us to commit for about twenty-four hours.

During those twenty-four hours, we found our new place. It was just a hotel for the night until we were able to find and move into an apartment. The rain was off and on and we were exhausted. We met Oleg walking through the courtyard of the hotel. He was standing there tall, in a suit, trench coat, and holding a black umbrella. He looked very sophisticated. He was there to help us with things in Vinnytsia while Irena was working with other families in other parts of the country. She went home that night with the taxi driver, and we were all alone. Just us and Oleg. After Oleg was done showing us to our room, he too would also leave. We had big plans for dinner. There was a restaurant right off the courtyard. I was so hungry by this point. Absolutely nothing was in English, and I just had to take a chance. I was so tired, I just picked something that sounded like it may be tasty. It was the smallest little plate of food. Apparently, I ordered from the appetizers. I gobbled it up and went back to our room.

Time for bed after an extremely long day. Both Tim and I fell asleep in an instant. Between jet lag and a long day, it wasn't too surprising. We ended up sleeping for eighteen hours! Both of us were asleep like logs the entire time. I barely remember the hotel because we slept just about the entire time we were there. It's a little scary waking up after that long, not knowing where you are, or how it got to be so late the following day. After a little bit of being awake, we got a call from Irina and Oleg was to take us to our new apartment.

We packed up our stuff yet again and off we went. We were truly living in suitcases up to this point. We pulled up to our new apartment, the place we would be living in over the next couple of months. It wasn't really anything special. A one-bedroom apartment, with one twin bed. The couch was able to be smushed together to create a full-size bed, just had to ignore the pole that would dig into my hip at night. There was a small kitchen with a two-person table tucked to the side. The bathroom was pink and had the laundry facilities next to the tub. The Wi-Fi connection was good when the owner of the apartment decided to pay the bill. We had a view of neighboring houses and a busy street. It will do. We weren't there to live in luxury. Soon we were left to ourselves, given strict instructions not to go out at night. With nothing left to do, we unpacked and made ourselves at home.

We headed to the Supermarket all by ourselves that night (before it got dark) to pick up some much-needed groceries. I'm a huge fan of Diet Coke, so I had to enter the world of Coca Cola Lite. We looked at the price of peanut butter and were extremely thankful we brought our own. It was almost $10 for one small tub. Looking at all the options of groceries was very intimidating. We didn't know what most of the meat was or anything on the shelves. We picked up some pasta noodles, but they didn't have a typical pasta sauce so we searched for a sauce that may be decent. We picked up bread which didn't have any preservatives so we needed to eat it quickly as it would go moldy fast. It was an experience, but as each shopping trip came along, we became a little more adventurous. Throughout our trip we tried what we thought was chicken, and ended up being what we believe was pigeon with all its innards still intact. We bought something else we thought was meat, but doing a Google translate on it once back to the apartment, turned out to be oatmeal pancakes with cheese. It was actually quite delicious when we sauteed it on the stove. Pasta became a staple for us. It was easy to make, and we always had left over for dinner the next night. Peanut butter sandwiches were also our go to, and the peanut butter lasted us about three weeks. We were more adventurous in the snack department. We enjoyed chocolate wafer cookies, seasoned popcorn, and a brand of chips that had so many varieties. My favorite was lobster. Sounds gross, smells off, but I soon became addicted to them.

Back at our apartment where we would go and spend the majority of our time. Irina called us the next day and asked the big question we'd been waiting for. "Would you like to start the process of adoption for Diana?" Yes! Absolutely, 100%. It's a little crazy to make such a big decision after just meeting her for fifteen minutes, but when you trust your heart, your heart will lead you in the right direction. Had we not had a connection with Diana, or we were unsure, we did have the option to go back to the SDA (after obtaining another appointment) and start the process over. They allowed for up to three children to be visited per family before you would need to head back home to the states.

At this point, a week has gone by, and we were just beginning to start the process in Ukraine. Most people we have read about were moving along much quicker than us. We would later see we would be delayed repeatedly for various reasons.

We were now moving forward with the adoption, which meant we were now allowed to visit Diana on our own at the orphanage every day. Each orphanage is different. Some have set times, some will welcome you at any time, and some don't allow daily visits. We were lucky enough to be able to visit daily from three to five o'clock.

Tim and I did not want to take a taxi every time we visited. It would add up in cost, plus we would have to call Irina each day to set one up for us. We like to find different ways of getting around. Trying to fit in, like we belong. We chose the tram. The tram was actually very convenient. We would have to walk about two blocks to catch it and it would drop us off about two blocks away from the orphanage. It was fairly cheap too.

Every day for the next several weeks we had the same ritual. We would stay at the apartment all day while Tim caught up on his work, then we would go to the orphanage to visit Diana, then come back to the apartment, and make dinner. We typically stayed up very late every night as we didn't have much to wake up for, so we got to sleep in. I can honestly say, this time in my life I had the most sleep. I guess you can say I was trying to get all my sleep in before I actually had a child.

When we would visit the orphanage, we would play with Diana for two hours straight. We would have the gym to ourselves. It was so cold in there, they didn't have the heat running, but we would get warmed up pretty quick. Diana loved having her Dad (Papa as she called him at the time), running after her on the mats. She loved coloring together and singing songs. She also loved grabbing my camera every time I tried to take a picture and she wanted to see. It was hard to get a good picture as usually it was her hand in front of the lens. When the weather allowed, we would go outside and play on the playground. One of her favorites was to look at the pictures we brought. Through pictures she was able to meet her grandparents, aunt, uncles, and cousins. She was able to see her two dogs that were waiting for her at home. She was able to see the house she would live in and her very own bedroom. She was so excited to head to America and start her life. We were anxiously awaiting as well. For those two straight hours a day, she was the center of attention and she loved it.

Every now and again, Irina would come back to Vinnytsia, or Oleg would take us to the Department, and we would need to sign more paperwork to get to the next step, and then the next, and then the one after that. Those days we typically couldn't go to the orphanage. I would wonder if she noticed we didn't come, if she was heartbroken we weren't there, if she felt abandoned. The next day we would visit and all would be right in the world again.

While two hours a day doesn't sound like a lot, it really meant so much to us and Diana. We had so much time to bond and figure out our own little family. We figured out how to communicate with each other when we didn't understand the other's languages. It really was a blessing. Much like when Tim and I had the opportunity to be in a long distant relationship. It doesn't feel like a blessing at the moment, but looking back, it was the opportunity most people don't get a chance for. All you're able to do is talk to each other, which builds the relationship and keeps it strong. At the orphanage we had to find ways to communicate together, which built our strong family bond. We learned to understand each other on another level. We taught her some English, she taught us some Ukrainian, we taught each other about family.

Chapter Seven

Each day came and went. We became more robotic as every day was practically the same. There was delay after delay. First, finding Diana in the beginning as mentioned before. Then there were delays with our paperwork from time to time, notaries were closed early, etc. Typically, it was said by many bloggers that the entire process in country would take around six weeks. For us, it was just about six weeks before we finally got our court date, and this was after we had to bribe the judge. Apparently, the only way to get a court date is with a bribe of chocolates and extra money. It was a long process, and no one seemed to care how long it was taking.

For me I was starting to stress out. I had to get back home to get back to work. We weren't wealthy by any means, and I was extremely lucky my job allowed me to take all my vacation time all at once. I built up 5 weeks in total before FMLA would kick in. The problem with FMLA is that you don't get paid, it just keeps your job secure. I was happy to be able to have that security, but we needed me to be working instead. Unfortunately, my job was not one of those that allowed maternity leave for adoptions.

We kept asking and asking Irina how much longer and she couldn't give us a straight answer. We had to book round trip tickets for our trip in order for Ukraine to even let us in the country. We knew we would have to possibly reschedule the return flight, but to not have any official dates yet was stressful. We just waited the best we could.

Finally, on October 18, 2003, we had our court date. Typically, with older children, they allow them to come to court, but unfortunately we didn't even see Diana that day at all. We put on our nice clothes, the same ones we wore to the SDA almost six weeks earlier. They were so baggy on us, it was unbelievable. I didn't realize how much weight we really lost until that day. We walked so much, had high stress levels, and were very picky about food. All the food we ate didn't have preservatives. It was the best weight loss program we ever had. Turns out in six weeks I had lost twenty-five to thirty pounds without even trying.

Irina picked us up for court. We took the taxi and waited outside for our case to be called. I don't know why I was so stressed about this day. Yes it was up to the judge to decide if we were at last going to be allowed to become a family, but there was no reason why it wouldn't go our way. As you can see, stress is the main theme of the entire adoption process. We sat there in the court room. There were witnesses to the right of the room, sitting there with an oversized doll. It was very confusing and very funny. They were talking amongst themselves, and Irina let us know it was the judge's first adoption case. I was a little leery as we were his guinea pig, but there was nothing I could do about it. Tim started giggling with the witnesses. He handles stress way differently than me. I had to kick him to keep his composure. As with the rest of the trip, no one spoke English in the courthouse either. I understood certain words like our names and our address as the judge read the verdict. Irina told us when to stand and sit. Finally, a smile came from the judge, and he ruled in our favor, as Irina translated that part to us.

It was official, we were a family!!! Well, sort of. By law, we had to wait out a ten-day period after the court ruling before we could take legal custody of Diana. During these ten days, the court could change their mind, or the birth mother could come forward to stop everything. In our case the birth mother's rights were severed four years earlier, so it wasn't much of a worry. However, during this waiting game, we were unable to get Diana ready. Meaning, we were unable to get her visa together. Unable to take her for her vaccinations. None of that. It was literally a hold time.

Tim and I made a very difficult decision. We decided for me to keep my original flight that was already booked and head home. Tim would stay in Ukraine by himself and finish up the process and bring our Diana home when all is done. I mentioned we didn't see Diana during our court day. The reason being was that court ran over our allowed meeting time. Unfortunately, I didn't get to see her again at all in Ukraine. My flight was scheduled in two days, and I was still very far from Kiev.

Once we got back to the apartment, I packed up all my things. I took as much home as possible to make it easier for Tim when it was his time to come back. The next day Irina called a taxi who took us to the train station and off I went. The train is an interesting experience. It stops for about a minute and so many people are pushing their way onto the train. You literally get lost in the sea of people. I had to kiss and hug Tim goodbye before the train got there and then grab all my luggage and rush to get on. It was late at night, and I had just a typical seat. Apparently I was sitting next to someone's friend, and she asked if I could switch seats with her. I was all by my lonesome, so of course I would, but even better, it was an upgraded seat in a quiet closed off section with just three other people. I sat back, tried to hold my tears back as I didn't want to leave both my husband and daughter behind, and tried to distract myself by playing Sudoku. The lady I sat next to knew English and she was a great distraction to me for the long three-hour train ride.

Once the train reached its destination in Kiev, I met up with Irina and the taxi driver. They dropped me at the airport. My flight wasn't for another eight hours, but I didn't want to get a hotel room. I just wanted to be left alone and not have to run around in the morning. I sat just outside security so I could get up and walk outside anytime I felt like it. It was getting cold as the automatic doors kept opening. I sat myself in a chair with my luggage as a foot stool. I tried to nap, but really didn't sleep at all. The night was very long, and I didn't have any communication with anyone. I was lonely, scared, depressed, and tired.

It was finally time for me to get passed security and head towards my plane. This flight including both connections was so much shorter than getting out there. I was just so tired, I slept almost the entire way back. If I wasn't sleeping I would keep to myself and watch some movies.

On my way back home, I connected both in Vienna, Austria and then Dulles International Airport in Washington, DC. Vienna wasn't a big deal, but we all had to get rescanned through security before being able to get to our connections. In Dulles, American soil, not only did I have to reclaim my bag to get it checked again, but I also had to go through customs. I didn't think it was a big deal, but when I was questioned on my trip in Ukraine, I answered that I was there for an adoption. TSA looked me up and down and questioned where my kid was. Luckily he believed me when I said Tim was still over there with her and I had to come back early.

Once in Dulles waiting for my next flight, I was able to enjoy some of the football game that was televised. I was excited to see they had it on all the tv's. Next stop...Phoenix! I was excited to get home, sleep in my own bed, and see my dogs.

My good friend picked me up from the airport. I allowed her to borrow my car while I was gone, plus she was the one house sitting for us. She drove me from Phoenix Sky Harbor to Mesa, where her apartment was. She had another mode of transportation at this time and made me drive the rest of the way home. I was so tired, but very happy to drive. It was a long six weeks since I even drove. I parked my car in the garage and could hear Hunter and Scout barking at the door. As soon as I opened the door, they were so incredibly excited to see me. I've never seen them this excited before. I opened the back door, and they ran in circles for a good half hour. Jumping on me, kissing me, and running with excitement some more. As sad as I was for who I left behind, leave it to the dogs to make you feel so much better.

Now that I was home, I decided to give myself one additional week off to get the house in order and get rid of my jet lag before returning. I had to wait a little bit anyways because I had to get a hold of Human Resources to cancel the rest of my FMLA and allow me to return to work. The first day I didn't do a whole lot, just recovered. I went out to Burger King for lunch, but they still had their breakfast menu up. I was so used to going to McDonald's when we were in Ukraine that out of habit I tried ordering a Big Mac. There was a long pause from the employee and then she said, "we don't have that here." I was ready to get angry because all I wanted was food before I went and got groceries and then realized it was a Whopper I needed to request.

Diana's room was pretty much in order. My mom flew out the fall before we went to Ukraine and helped me decorate. At the time we didn't know if we would have a boy or a girl, so we left it very gender neutral, in blue and green dots with different size and texture letters of the alphabet on the wall. I figured that would be helpful to any child coming home not knowing the English alphabet. I did, however, add some pink to her room before she came home. I added her name to the wall as well. Just the little touches to make her feel at home once the day finally came. Her bathroom was just plain white, so I had plenty of time to girl it up. I made a ladybug shower curtain and painted ladybugs on the wall. Projects like these were therapy for me, knowing she would be coming home soon, and keeping me busy so I wouldn't be so anxious for the day. At this point, we didn't even know how long Tim and Diana would be over there. We just knew it was a ten-day waiting period before anything else could move along.

Chapter Eight

      That last chapter was where my story ended in Ukraine. However, Diana and Tim were still there. Tim's story picks up just as I had left on the train. The taxi driver that took us to the train station claimed he had to leave and was not able to take Tim back to the apartment. Tim thought it was no big deal and decided to try to walk back by himself. Keep in mind the taxi ride was at least a half hour away, so walking would take much longer. Streets he knew were shut down, he ended up going through neighborhoods he never saw before. He kept making wrong turns. It was very dark and getting late at night. He finally got himself so lost that he decided to call Irina. Irina didn't know where he was, as GPS wasn't on this type of cell phone yet. He had to find a store and have someone take the phone and let Irina know where he was. Thankfully he did find someone that could help her. She called a taxi, and he was saved. He was literally a five-minute walk away, he just got very turned around. He ended up getting back to the apartment just as I was getting off the train. He asked Irina not to tell me about him being lost as he knew I would worry. In fact, he didn't even tell me about it for a few months. He was right though; I would have been more worried than I needed to be.

Tim continued to visit Diana at the orphanage. She would look in the sky and point to an airplane and say, "Mama". She knew I went home. But she also knew she would get to come home soon as well.

Tim did a lot of the same things we did before. Worked, went to the orphanage, grocery shopped, and on occasion went out with Oleg. Finally, the ten waiting days were over and now Diana was officially part of our family. This was go time. Time to get her passport and visa, time to get her immunizations. It was slow moving at first, but then the process really sped along. When all was said and done, we realized why it sped up so fast and why they allowed her to go to America without getting her immunization that they claim they did not have. Three weeks later, Ukraine was at war, and the Ukrainians clearly needed to get Tim and Diana out of the country beforehand.

Tim had to travel with Irina to Diana's birthplace in order to obtain her birth certificate. He was made to wait in the car the entire time they were stopped there. He was able to see it was a small town of only a couple streets. Some trailers for houses along with the government building, was all that was there. From there they were able to get her new birth certificate issued with her new middle and last name and both of us listed as her parents. The passport and visa were expedited. Before we knew it they were rushing them out of the country and Tim was finding flights to come home at last. He was there for a total of nine weeks.

November 6, 2013, Tim and Diana boarded their flight from Kiev, Ukraine to Phoenix, Arizona making stops in Russia and JFK in New York. He did not have as relaxing of a flight home as I did. He took Diana to the restroom at the Russian airport and by the time they were done, he realized the entire plane was waiting for them to board. They finally boarded and were on their way back to the United States. Diana had to use the restroom once again. Tim allowed her to go in by herself as airplane restrooms are so tiny. She managed to lock herself in there and couldn't get out. He had to find someone who spoke Ukrainian or Russian to help guide her out. Once deplaned in JFK they had to grab their luggage and go through customs. Diana saw a bag she really wanted. It was a Hello Kitty bag. What eight-year-old wouldn't want that. She started screaming and Tim couldn't control her as she didn't understand why she couldn't have that bag. Security came and took Tim and Diana into separate rooms. Tim was an English speaker and had a child with him that didn't know the language. It looked suspicious. Talk about intimidating. He was finally in America and right away treated like he was a criminal. After he explained the situation and they were certain he wasn't a child trafficker, they let them move along.

November 7th came and the anticipation of them coming home was through the roof. I couldn't concentrate at work. I was over the moon that I was just a few hours away from picking them up. After work, I stayed at my friend's house so I wouldn't have to drive back and forth so much as I worked near the airport. They came with me for support and to video and take pictures of Diana and Tim arriving home. We were a small but mighty welcoming crew. Finally, their plane had landed, and we stared at the exit waiting for them to walk through. There they were, they made it! Diana saw me and came running towards me and gave me the biggest hug ever. I was crying and she was patting my back. A moment no one could ever take away from me. Tim looked exhausted and he was so happy to be home. I had made him his favorite cheese sandwich, some chips, and had a Pepsi all ready for him once we made it back to my car. I made Diana a special late-night dinner as well. We finally headed home as a family of three.

One of the great things about an international adoption, at least at the time, is once Diana touched foot in America, she was considered a U.S. citizen since both her dad, and I are.

Once home, the dogs were excited. They didn't know who this strange kid was in their house, but they accepted her right away. Due to the picture book, we had given her, she already knew who Hunter and Scout were. Tim was ready to head to bed and I elected to stay up and be on alert with Diana. I showed her the bedroom. We got her all ready for bed. All night I kept waking up as I heard noises coming from her room. Time after time, I put her back in bed. She wasn't tired, she had all new toys, a new room she didn't have to share with anyone. I couldn't really blame her for not wanting to sleep, but I was starting to get very tired.

Morning came and we had breakfast and let her watch some cartoons. We wanted to have an easy day and ease her into her new life. I took her to the park so Tim could have a little more peace and quiet. She loved going down the slide and attempting the monkey bars. We came home for lunch and not long after, she fell asleep half on the couch and half on the floor. Her exhaustion finally hit, and she couldn't stay awake any longer. Sometimes I would have to pinch myself to make sure I wasn't dreaming, and this was real. Our first day as parents in our own country and in our own home, was a success.

Chapter Nine

Throughout our stay in both Kiev and Vinnytsia, we had plenty of adventures and plenty of time to create memories. While many of our days were mundane, there were definitely stand out stories. Throughout this chapter, I will take a break from talking about the adoption itself and talk about some of our favorite, and not so favorite memories.

When we were in Kiev, we were still very new to being in Ukraine. We were a nervous wreck. I wish we didn't live in such fear the whole time, but I was always one to not let my guard down. Tim and I had the chance to walk around Kiev a bit on our own. We headed to downtown Kiev which wasn't very far to walk. It was such a beautiful city. The statues standing tall, the buildings so old, the history so vibrant. We didn't have much to do in the city so for a better part of our time we sat and people watched. We watched this one group of guys for a while. Granted, we couldn't understand what they were saying, but by their actions, still to this day, we are positive they were in the mob. Then we would turn our eyes to the escalator (there was a small shopping strip underground) and we would see the babushkas. The grandma's who would wear scarves around their heads. The tall building had a sign of 17 degrees Celsius on the day we were there. We had to go back to Google and figure out what that meant in Fahrenheit. It was 62.6 degrees Fahrenheit in case you were curious. There were men on bicycles that would deliver sushi and pizza, and across the street there were people dressed in character costumes acting as minions. It truly felt like a whole other world.

We decided to have food that we were familiar with and headed to the McDonalds nearby. I never saw a McDonalds so big in my life. Not only was it large, it was also very crowded. The employee asked us how many people we had as we held up two fingers to communicate. They were seating people at tables. They sat us with an Englishman that was visiting the country to watch a soccer match. It was fantastic. It was probably about five days at this point that we heard someone speaking English that we could understand, and we had great conversations with him until he was done eating. We ordered Big Mac's because they were the easiest to order without any translation issues. We sat and enjoyed our meal before heading back to our apartment.

In Kiev we were with Galina often as that was her territory. We will never believe our eyes walking to the SDA appointment. She had all our paperwork with her that we sent while we were still at home. She had it in one hand and would talk while using that hand. We couldn't hear much of what she was saying as she flung our many months' worth of work all around. Thankfully she didn't drop any and nothing flew, but I literally felt my heart skip a beat. To her it was just another case, to us it was the most important papers we've ever had.

Galina took us on a walking tour in another part of Kiev that we hadn't been to. She showed us tall buildings and intricate statues. We had no idea what anything was as she was hard to understand, but she insisted we take our pictures with them. To this day, we have all these pictures and no idea what they are, except a good memory.

Irina was a five-foot slender young woman who was sweet and a bit feisty. She was straight and to the point without sugar coating anything. A good quality when going through something as tough and stressful as an international adoption. She would enter a building and push her tiny self through the crowd. Tim and I would try to keep up with her, but she was always so far ahead. She never cared about other people who were standing in a line. When we would give her a look to resemble, "the lines starts back here," she would tell us that it was okay because we had important business. It happened at the bank, it happened at the department, it happened at the notary. Everywhere we went her business was more important than anyone else's. It was good for us as we didn't have to wait as long, but I wonder what the thoughts those other people had? Is that typical behavior? If that happened in America, I couldn't even imagine. There would be so many angry people.

Most of our experiences happened in Vinnytsia as that is where we spent the majority of our time. Oleg became a friend of ours and often offered to show us around. One night we met up with him and his daughter, Nastya. We met at the department, which we were very familiar with as we had to go there many times to sign papers. This man we were used to seeing dressed in suits and ties came walking up in a track suit and sneakers. We almost didn't recognize him at first in the crowd of people walking down the sidewalk. We weren't sure what we were planning on doing that night, but it was dark already. It was okay for us to be out as we were with someone that knew the area and had our best interests in mind. We waited for a bus and when it came I still didn't have my money ready as I didn't know how much it would be. I ended up holding up the whole line as I couldn't understand what they were telling me. Nastya told the bus driver and passengers behind us that it was okay. We were "Americanski's". Probably the most embarrassing time. She was only twelve and making excuses for us being so slow. We finally boarded the bus and off we went. We got to our destination and then had to walk a bit to the Roshen light show. We had no idea what we were in for. But after that embarrassing moment on the bus, this would end up being the best night. Roshen is a chocolate company like Hershey in America. They put on the most spectacular show on the water with lights. It's so hard to actually describe it. I would say some of the light shows at Disney parks could probably come close, but this was even better than those.

They played videos through the falling water and had songs blasting in the crowds. My absolute favorite song to hear was "We are the Champions," by Queen. The entire crowd went wild. Everyone singing every single lyric. I was amazed. Very little English spoken by the majority of these spectators, yet singing this English song was done perfectly. What an experience it was.

As I mentioned in the chapter previous, we decided taking the tram was a good idea for us to get from our apartment to the orphanage. We don't mind public transportation and prefer it over other means. About day three of going to the orphanage by ourselves, I took out the money prior to leaving the apartment. This was the first time I was super prepared and gave Tim his money rather than just holding onto it for both of us. He pocketed the change, and off we went. We had a typical walk to the station. The tram came. People were everywhere. I waited for those to come off before I got on. Somehow Tim didn't see me get on. He waited for a moment looking around for me. In that moment, the tram left. Heart sinking again. He got left at the station and I was alone on the tram. I rushed to the back of the tram to see him there waiting and not knowing what had just happened. I didn't know what to do. We had no way to communicate with each other. Do I get off at the next stop and jump on the next tram that comes by in hopes he is on that one? Do I stay and get off at the orphanage stop and hope he does the same? Do I walk to the orphanage so we're not late for the meeting time with Diana? I was very thankful something told me to give him his money, otherwise he would've been stuck. I opted to get off at the orphanage and hoped he remembered where that was as we were still new to this tram system. I waited and waited for the next one to come around. Finally, it pulled up. I looked around at everyone getting off, then there he was. I've never been so happy to see Tim in my life. Just like in the movies, we just ran into each other's arms. It felt like slow motion. We stood hugging for what seemed like forever and finally walked off hand in hand to the orphanage. It was the scariest part of our journey, and I will forever be thankful that we thought the same and that I gave him money. From that point on we had back up plans as to what we should do if we ever become separated. I suggest to everyone else to have these plans in place before it actually happens.

Tim and I were hungry for some good old American food. In other words, McDonald's as that was the only thing recognizable to us in that region. We made a deal with ourselves. On Wednesdays we would be able to go to McDonald's if we walked home from the orphanage. The McDonald's wasn't all that far from the orphanage, so we had no problem walking there afterwards. We would go, eat Big Macs, and relax a bit before starting our walk home. I believe we figured it to be a whole three miles from start to finish. One day I was brave and ordered nuggets rather than a Big Mac. Unfortunately, we didn't realize they charge for sauce until after we received our food. The nuggets were so good. So different from the ones in America. They had a lot of flavoring, and I could tell there was pepper on each one. It really makes one realize how food is so different from one country to the next even though it claims it's the same thing.

McDonald's wasn't the only time that we decided to walk to or from the orphanage. We actually did it on several occasions. Could be where some of the weight loss came from as well. It was a very enjoyable walk, nothing scary about it. In fact, it was such a great city, we often talked about how we wish there was a city like it in America. I'm sure there is, but we don't know about it. On our walks we would see squirrels climbing trees, a mom and a kid carrying a red balloon walking down the path of bare trees, a turtle made out of the bushes at a nearby bar. It was a carefree moment while walking. One day it even got cold enough that we started seeing a few snow flurries. By the time we got to the orphanage, we were not tired. We were energized to keep up with our daughter. Even if we were tired, we couldn't show it as she waited all day for those two hours to come.

There was one time near the beginning of us living in Vinnytsia that we decided to walk. We walked through a park. It had a giant "I Love Vinnytsia" sign where we just had to have our picture taken. We knew the night before there was a concert in the green area. As we walked through the park, we noticed some money was left behind. Just the coins, called hryvnia. Tim picked it up as he does with change back home. As he was picking it up, we saw more, and more, and more. It was everywhere. We collected our winnings and headed back to the apartment. We noticed a lot of times when we would go out walking we would find some, whether it was one coin or several. Each time we would pick it up. It became a challenge for us. How many hryvnia could we find. We never spent any of it. In fact, it remained our souvenir from our trip. We were on the tram one day and heard a coin drop near the door. We went out separate exits so one of us could find where it went and pick it up. There was one in the street that after days of trying to get, we realized it was stuck in the tar of the street and would never be able to come out. We would find some in the flowerpots, sidewalks, and stores. It's like people just disposed of all coins. We loved our hryvnia hunting and gave us a purpose during our stay. If we just wanted to stay in, the other would mention the hryvnia's that may be out there, and we would miss out if we stayed in. It really got us through the day. When I was through security at the airport in Kiev on my way back home, the airport was still empty. I saw in the distance hryvnia stacked at least three inches high on a chair armrest. I was so excited but wanted to remain casual. I went to grab the stack and the coins fell everywhere dinging off things making noise in the quiet environment. I quickly hurried to pick it all up and put it away. I couldn't wait to tell Tim about my find. Our goal was to hit the equivalent to $20 USD. We ended up surpassing it with my airport find and Tim's last three weeks there. Now a days with the currency exchange it wouldn't be worth that much, but to us it's priceless. To this day, we have all our prize-winning hryvnia on display in a shadow box. It will never be spent.

I mentioned earlier that Tim was lucky enough to work the entire nine weeks he was away. There were only two vacation days he ended up taking: travel day and court day. Since he was working, it kept us in the apartment more often. I felt safe there, but there were times I wanted to venture out, but obviously not on my own. There's only so much internet surfing one can do before they get completely stir crazy. I like to be crafty, so I found a project for myself. It did require me to go out of the apartment by myself, but I stayed nearby. I decided to take pictures of architecture letters, in other words, find something on a building or in a park, or in a hallway that represented a letter of the alphabet. I would find the shape of an 'I' on a railing and take a picture. I did this for the entire alphabet. It was a great challenge and something that allowed me to pass time. I would go out while Tim was working and head to the nearby park. The park was so unusual to the parks back home. Everything was made of recycled materials. Old tires were cut up and used as the park border, old pipes were incorporated into the equipment. Everything was so colorful too. The brightest of pinks and purples, blues like the sky. It was so very pretty. It was also a great place to find the letters I needed. By the end of my trip, I was successful in finding each one and I later put some together in a collage to spell out our last name.

Another way to pass my time if it was dark or rainy outside would be through the internet. I did have my laptop computer with me, which I was so happy I brought. I was able to email my family and friends to tell them what was going on and what the next step we were waiting for would be. We also had Skype which was perfect to see the people we were missing. The internet connection wasn't always the best so it did get frustrating, but we dealt with it the best we could. I would email my work friends while they were working as they were eight hours behind us. It was a great distraction for me, and for them to make the workday go quicker. It felt like people were there for us and they cared. It made a world of difference.

Another thing to occupy myself was watching tv. There were no channels in English, but I did find TLC, which I was surprised about. They were airing shows I knew and have seen before. Craft shows, reality shows, etc. The kicker is while they dubbed Ukrainian over, if you listened really closely, you could hear the English in the background. I would turn up the volume a bit and tune out the dubbing and manage to enjoy a whole bunch of shows. My favorite was one about animal cops. It was based in Maricopa County, which is the county over from us in Arizona. I was living all the way across the world and watching a show from just down the road from our house. We didn't have all the streaming service options like we do now, or that would've been my go-to. Every Sunday night, very late at night, we would pull up the computer and attempt to stream the NFL game. It was the morning game as we laid in bed struggling to stay awake for the first half. The times we managed to stream the game without problems, we were able to stay up a little later. It wasn't always a success.

Every weekend we had big plans, just the two of us. Friday nights there always seemed to be a police officer sitting at the bend in the road just past our apartment. We would grab chairs, or sometimes just stand, and watch out our window, yelling "busted", if he pulled someone over. He pulled so many people over, it was a game to see if we could call out the right car. On Saturday nights, there were always fireworks going off somewhere. The citizens always celebrated with fireworks, whether it was a soccer match win or a wedding, or even a birthday party. They put on the greatest shows, and we could almost always see them from our window.

Our window looked out to a neighborhood. Tim and I would make up stories about how the residents had to be rich as they were very nice-looking houses. We would see them come and go with hockey bags and their gated driveway locked behind them. We made up a story of him having an underground hockey rink in his basement and he was training to be an NHL star. There was one house that was fun to keep our eyes on throughout our entire stay. We just referred to them as "the guys". The guys were remodeling the outside of their home. It started off as a gorgeous brick house and we watched every day see it transform. They covered the brick with some material like dry wall and then painted over it to have no resemblance of that brick ever existing. We would look out and see them working away day in and day out. There were two of them. One guy was younger, we claimed it was the owner's son-in-law. He did most of the work. The other guy we assumed was the owner of the house. He would look on and give his supervising guidance, walk to the other side of the roof if he saw someone he knew and carry on a conversation, then walk back, and give more guidance. It was very rare that he picked up a tool to work. For about four weeks, we watched as the house transformed. We actually took pictures, not of the house, but of the beautiful trees in the background, when we first started living there, and then again when Tim was leaving for Kiev. In both pictures the house happened to be there. It was awesome to be reminded of what it looked like prior. For the record, I believe the house looked better before all the hard work they put into it.

The longer we stayed in Ukraine, the more comfortable we became. We were learning some Ukrainian, learning how to read Ukrainian, and going out more often on our own. And really on our own. Tim is a teacher, yes, he taught online before it was cool. There was one day he had an amazing opportunity. He was able to go to Nastya's classroom and teach English for the day. All the students were so excited to see an American and use their English skills. They asked him all sorts of questions like silly laws we have never heard. One example was, if it was true that in Alabama it was illegal for cattle to cross the street on a certain day. Yep, those are the "facts" that are being taught in other countries about America. While there, the students were also very excited to teach him Ukrainian and teach him how to spell his name. Definitely an experience that will live on forever.

While Tim was at the school, I wanted to visit Diana as we had to miss the past couple days due to going to notaries. Before I went, I was in a shopping mood and knew the grocery store had some clothes I could pick up for her. I just wanted to pick up a couple t-shirts and underwear for whenever she could come home. I shopped, then went to the register. Apparently one of the shirts didn't have a tag on it. The cashier asked me something, I'm assuming it was how much it said it was, and I unfortunately didn't understand her. I advised her I speak English and she threw her hands in the air and stormed off to find out the price. Right there I felt so small. I knew basic words at this point, but not enough to carry out an actual sentence or to understand one. I soon felt how people that don't speak English in America must feel. It was so degrading. After my purchase, I said thank you in Ukrainian and left. I then took the tram by myself and walked to the orphanage. We had a good visit, nothing out of the ordinary. On the tram back towards the apartment, I passed a park that we always went by. However, this time was different. As I looked out the window, I noticed a group of people gathering. I looked even closer and saw Nazi's in full uniform. Suddenly, I felt scared again. I honestly never knew they were still out there. In history class, they taught us about them, but not that they were still in existence. When Tim came back, I quickly told him about it, and he saw them too, but they were already marching when he saw them. Oleg was with Tim and treated it like it was no big deal. Apparently, it was just a normal thing to see there. It opened our eyes to the world we still live in.

We weren't always stuck inside the apartment. We did go out on occasion as well. We became close friends with Oleg and his daughter and are still social media friends to this day. One night he offered to take us out to have a bit of fun. It was definitely much needed. We met up with him and some of his friends to go bowling. I was excited because I used to be a bowler when I was in high school and haven't gone in such a long time. I laughed so hard when Oleg would throw the bowling ball in the air almost hitting the ceiling for it to come crashing down, rolling, and ending up in the gutter. He tried so hard, and we had such a great time. Tim and I both have been craving some American food. We asked Oleg if the bar had hamburgers. Just what every American needs. He talked to the bar manager and got us excited they were going to make something special just for us. Now, Americans tend to have large portion sizes for meals and our mindset was set on a big juicy burger. Out it came; two tiny palm sized "hamburgers". They were small pieces of buttered bread with a piece of pepperoni and that was it. Oleg didn't understand the problem, "It's bread and it's meat, it's hamburger." I started thinking they didn't know what a hamburger truly was, but then realized they had McDonald's and some other American restaurants, surely they would know. We were up for some adventurous foods, but sometimes you just crave that ground beef burger.

Speaking of food, have you ever tried to order a pizza in another country, which was named Chicago Pizza? Well, that was an experience to say the least. We passed this restaurant repeatedly while riding on the tram and one day decided we should try it. There was no one in the restaurant but employees, so we walked right up to the counter ready to order. Having a translator of sorts would have really come in handy here. We tried ordering a large cheese pizza. Yes, we are not very adventurous with our food choices. We've had our share of pierogi's, potato pancakes, sausage, and the like while there, but sometimes those American cravings hit. Originally from Chicago myself, I didn't think this would go wrong. They did have an English menu printed out, which did help, but they couldn't understand that we just wanted cheese and sauce without any other toppings. It literally took us thirty minutes to place our order. When they delivered our food you could just see the hesitation in their eyes thinking it was screwed up. It was perfect. Not the best pizza I've had by any means, but it was at least how we requested it. I mentioned the English menu. I was in shock as to what toppings they offered. Things like liver and kidneys. That is absolutely no Chicago pizza that I've ever had.

Living in Ukraine for six and nine weeks, we had to do the typical household chores. Washing dishes, cleaning up the apartment, and of course laundry. There was no way we were going to pack six weeks of clothes to take with us. Laundry sounds so typical, but it was a little odd for us. First, our washing machine was in the bathroom next to the shower. In our first apartment we were at, it was in the kitchen which was just as odd to me but came to find out that was more normal. Secondly, we're used to more modern conveniences like dryers. It was the first time in my life I had to hang my clothes to dry. The clothesline was outside, but I didn't have any clips or pins, plus the weather wasn't always the greatest, so it wasn't the greatest option. We had that spare bedroom that was only used if Irena had spent the night. We laid out towels across the floor and every bit of laundry across the bedroom. It was chilly in the apartment and sometimes took days for clothes to get dry. We soon came to find out our laundry detergent didn't have any sort of fabric softener. It wasn't horrible for jeans and t-shirts, but it was very hard on the socks. By the end of our trip, I ended up throwing away all the socks we brought as they all ended up with holes. At least it was less to pack, I suppose.

Things didn't always go without injury. With six weeks in a foreign country, we were bound to end up with some silly painful stories. Our bed was really a couch that was pushed together. It was so uncomfortable. We got as used to it as we could but couldn't get over the bar in the middle. My hip would dig into the bar so badly that I had to put a pillow under my hip to cushion the blow. It was so bad that for weeks my hip was bruised.

While at the orphanage for one of our visits, we were able to go outside. It was a chilly day, but with everyone bundled up, they allowed it. There were other kids playing outside and Tim saw they were playing soccer. He used to play soccer when he was a kid, so without hesitation he asked the preteens if he could join them. They were so excited because most adults wouldn't do that. I was with Diana in a corner in the yard as he played with everyone. It was going great, until his body realized he wasn't so young anymore. One really good kick of the soccer ball and down he went. His knee just buckled. He yelled for me to come over. Tim's body doesn't react well to excruciating pain and he kept talking to me in hopes he wouldn't pass out. I did not react well. I didn't know what to do. He couldn't walk, I was responsible for Diana at the time, there were kids checking if he was okay, and his face was turning white. Luckily there was one kid who thought quickly and ran in and got a bag of ice. With so many people around, Tim was able to shake off the possibility of passing out and got up to hobble to a bench. For days, maybe even weeks, he was in so much pain. We were too scared to visit a hospital and had too many things we needed to accomplish where we wouldn't have time to give into the pain. I drugged him up on some ibuprofen and hoped for the best. We are almost positive he tore a ligament as he heard the tear just before he went down. Thankfully he made a full recovery, and it hasn't been much of an issue since.

There was another incident when we were playing outside. This time it was only Tim, Diana, and me. Diana was running through the playground with no care in the world and then just started screaming. My motherly instincts kicked in and I ran so fast over to her to see what the matter was. She pointed to her hand. In the palm of her hand was a stinger to a bee. She was stung. I managed to get the stinger out. She was screaming so loud even with me comforting her that we ended up running her back inside the orphanage for them to take a look. I felt like a little bit of a failure as we had to rely on them to fix her up, but they had the tools. The icepack, the band aid, and the language. We went home that night feeling a bit defeated, but the next day we visited, Diana was all smiles again. The nice part was we quickly learned she was not allergic to bees. Thank goodness too because she's been stung two other times since.

My grandmother was a big supporter of ours and knew we were looking into adoption. Unfortunately, she passed away only two months into the process. I always felt like she was guiding us and with us while we were in Ukraine. I hold onto that every day. Diana was meant to be our child. The SDA wasn't even going to show us her file, but yet hers was the one that kept falling out of the binder and finally placed on the table. I always felt like butterflies were a sign from my grandma. Anytime I needed a sign that she was watching over us after speaking to her, I would see a single butterfly flutter by. When we were in the playground one day with Diana we saw a beautiful butterfly. I didn't think much of it at first even though it was way too cold for butterflies to be out. However, it landed on the playground right next to us and just stood there. It landed on Diana, then Tim, and me. The butterfly would stick around for a good five minutes before it flew off. I felt like everything was going to be good. That no matter how hard it may feel, we were meant for each other, and it would be okay. I felt such power that day. The first year Diana was home, maybe even longer, I kept seeing butterflies. I started wondering if it was just in my mind that I was trying to justify why they would be around, but I didn't care, I felt at peace. When my grandfather passed away a couple years later, suddenly I would start seeing two butterflies together. Coincidence? I don't think so. I like to think that my grandma wanted so bad to be able to help us, that she was able to help in more ways than I could have imagined.

Chapter Ten

Diana was home at last. We didn't have much for her in terms of clothes, just a few hand-me-downs I was able to get from a friend of a friend. I was sitting at home one day on a Saturday, ready to go out, when Tim told me I needed to stay. I didn't understand, but I stayed home as he never requests anything like that. He pulled out the computer and placed it on the table. He then turned-on Skype. I was a bit confused. I walked over to the computer, and I couldn't believe my eyes. All my family in Illinois were gathered around a table and they had a makeshift baby shower for us. There were silly party games, food (which looked tasty), and I had a friend come over that brought over tons of gifts. Gifts received at her house so it would remain a surprise. It was fantastic. Not only did my sister and mom pull off a surprise shower, but it was a long-distance surprise. We received so many clothes and toys and Diana was able to meet everyone all at once through the computer. I will be forever thankful to my family for pulling that together.

Since Diana was officially home, we had to truly register her as an American citizen. She was a US citizen since she came home, however, we had to apply for her social security number. Another thing we did was not necessary, however, we felt it was. We had her Ukrainian birth certificate with us listed as her parents, however, it was obviously all in Ukrainian. We applied for a US birth certificate. It would be a lot easier with applying for different things in her future with something written in English with the appropriate seal. Technically it's a certificate of foreign birth. It was optional, but a must for us.

We had to register her for school within a certain time frame. I don't know why we felt so rushed. I think it was because Tim is a teacher and we needed to follow all the rules to a t. I never wanted to send her to our neighborhood school as there were several other choices around. However, it felt like that was our only option since we didn't really know where she stood on the education level.

Tim was emailing the school back and forth while he was in Ukraine, and we felt more comfortable sending her there. We didn't know what grade level to even put her in, so we went with our best guess of second grade since she was eight years old.

The first day of school was soon upon us, about two weeks after adjusting to at home life. She was so excited to go. I was so excited she would have the opportunity to meet other kids and hopefully make some new friends. It was scary sending her, my heart hurt thinking about what might go wrong as she's a little kid who knew only a handful of English words. While in

Ukraine, Tim and I had each other speaking the same language, for Diana, it's just her in this scary new world.

The day before Diana started school, the students had lesson on Ukraine to allow them to understand her country. Everyone in the classroom was so welcoming. They had her desk all picked out and a name tag ready to go that she could color. They introduced themselves to her and she had the biggest smile on her face. It was time for us to head out, and I didn't know what else to do. I took the day off for this and I can't see her again until three in the afternoon. I had all emotions going through me, I was worried, I was sad, I was happy, I was just an emotional wreck. We picked her up and turned out she had a great day!

As the days and weeks went by, however, we kept getting notes and calls from the school. They thought she was going to stab someone when she walked around the classroom with scissors. She would have a melt down because she didn't understand what was going on in class. She would hit a boy because he got in her face. It wasn't going well at all. The newness of her wore off and it felt like the school was starting to go against us. The school, along with us, decided to send her to first grade instead. It was a hard decision, but it quickly became clear that she never learned the basics. She didn't know numbers, she didn't know letters, even the Ukrainian ones, and she just needed to get that proper start. As it turned out, I knew a first-grade teacher at that school, and she offered to take her in her classroom. I felt at ease and thought this would be a better fit for her.

With school under way and Diana starting to settle in, her uncle from Texas was going to drive out for the Thanksgiving holiday. Since we didn't have any family in our state, this would be the first relative she would meet in person.

Diana was so excited to meet Uncle Joe. By now her English was getting a little better already. Kids pick up languages so much faster than adults can. He arrived while Tim and I were making dinner. Joe decided to take Diana to the park and play some wiffle ball catch. Not more than five minutes later, they came walking into the house; Diana screaming her head off and her face full of blood. I ran to her and got her calmed down and cleaned up. Apparently, her hand and eye coordination were not all there. She got hit smack dab in the nose with the wiffle ball. Joe felt bad, but to this day we will still credit him with being the very first person, and probably only guest, to break our kid in such a short amount of time. She was fine and eventually calmed down. She still loves her Uncle Joe.

Diana's first Thanksgiving was a success (minus the bloody nose). She was thrilled to have so much food to chow down on. Having a child straight from the orphanage can be tough with unveiling their traumas. Food issues were a major problem for her and probably will be for her whole life. Kids from orphanage living tend to have food issues because they're unsure of what their next meal will be and they typically are only given a tiny amount of food. I've heard of parents finding empty wrappers in their child's bedroom from food they hid away. Diana was never that sneaky. She just never knew when to stop eating. If she saw food, she would take it. If she saw others with food, especially fellow students, she would either ask them for some or steal it from them. She has been known to search the trash can at her school cafeteria and find pizza that was thrown away, grab it, and eat it. She wasn't hungry, we gave her everything she needed, but the trauma was still there and very persistent. She is now a young adult, and still struggles with food. She will eat breakfast at home and then go to school and eat another breakfast. It's gone on for months before figuring it out. I don't ever want to comment on a teenage girl's weight, but that was my key indicator. Her tummy was starting to grow. Diana will always lie when confronted, but unfortunately for her, we have a good relationship with her teachers and were able to figure it out quickly.

Back to her first few months. Diana's grandma and grandpa, my parents, were able to fly out to Arizona the first weekend in December. We were able to have an early Christmas celebration and grandparents were able to meet their newest granddaughter. Big hugs were had. Diana already knew them from seeing their pictures while we were in Ukraine and talking with them on Skype and over the phone. She opened her presents and received an

American Girl Doll from her grandpa, plus gift certificates to buy so many clothes for the doll. At this point, she just loved dolls. She mothered them and spoiled them. There was also a very large box that was shipped to our house. It was from her aunt, cousins, grandma, and grandpa. When she opened it, there it was. A large barbie dream house, that grandpa would have to put together before his visit was up. She became such a spoiled kid, but not in a bad way. Diana's first eight years of life were not the best of starts. She had to share everything while at the orphanage, and for the first time in her life, she was able to have her very own toys. She had every right to be spoiled for once.

Uncle Joe came back to visit during the actual Christmas holiday. This time he didn't break our kid. He visited the most out of everyone. She formed a close relationship with him right away. Tim and I usually spent the holidays alone, so it was nice to have family come and visit. As we all know, they were there for Diana and not for us, but it was still great to see everyone.

For New Years we celebrated by having a balloon pop day. Once I came home from work, she was able to pop one balloon an hour starting at noon. Inside each balloon I put an activity for her to do to pass the time until midnight. It would help her stay up really late and not be bored. There were activities in there like riding her bike, going to the park, playing some basketball, and more calm activities as the night went on that would keep her inside. Things like coloring, playing a game, playing with her dolls, etc. It was such a big hit we continued to do this every year until she was about sixteen. At that point, she just wanted to play on her phone and talk to her friend.

The following August, on my birthday weekend in fact, we got a call from Tim's brother Matthew. Joe was in a car accident after having a heart attack in the Walmart parking lot. It would be a good day or two until Matthew and Tim's mom were able to fly out to Texas and would take us only six hours to do the road trip. We quickly packed up our stuff and headed out to the hospital in El Paso. Joe was in stable condition, but in the ICU. Because Diana was still so young, she was unable to visit him, so we had to go in his room separately. Good thing we brought activity books for her to work through.

Late that night, Matthew and their mom arrived. It wasn't exactly the way we wanted Diana to meet her other uncle or her Grandmom, but we were thankful to have the opportunity to see them much earlier than we had intended. Her Grandmom reserved adjoining hotel rooms for the weekend, and they had a blast together. It was the first time I've seen my mother-in-law so happy. They would march in and out of the rooms together blowing horns and playing maracas. She gave Diana countless hugs and made sure she knew she loved her. Matthew would tease Diana by hiding her Cabbage Patch Kid from her and send Diana searching until she found it.

It was a tough weekend due to the circumstances, however it was a great visit that we otherwise would not have had. We only stayed the weekend and headed back home to get back to work and school. Joe needed some extra help after he was released from the hospital, so Matthew and my mother-in-law stayed much longer and moved Joe back to Philadelphia with them. It was nice having Joe nearby in Texas and him coming to visit when Diana came home. Now, all our family is much further away.

Chapter Eleven

When Diana was home for about seven months, we decided to plan a big get together with my side of the family. My sister, Kelly, her husband, and her five kids drove cross country from Chicago to our house. We had a great time celebrating Diana's nineth birthday. She didn't have any friends to have a birthday party with, so it was great we had people to come over and celebrate with. They all stayed at our house for a few days. It was fantastic chaos.

A few days later, we jumped into two different cars and headed to Irvine, California. My aunt and one of her kids live there. My mom flew into California and joined the fun. All of us stayed in my aunt's house for a couple days. We all headed to Disneyland as a big group with matching t-shirts and everything. It was a great trip had by all.

It was a big trip for Diana. She got to meet her aunt and cousins in person and meet her great aunt and another cousin as well. Plus, she was able to go to the happiest place on Earth. She feared a lot of the rides and would cry when something popped out and scared her. Fantasyland was definitely more her speed.

The night before we headed to Disneyland I overheard part of a conversation between my mom and my aunt (her sister). It caused my mom to have a discussion with my sister, myself, and my mom. Due to some circumstances, my parents were going to get divorced after nearly forty years of marriage. I was flabbergasted. I took it the hardest as I was more of a daddy's girl and just wanted to see him. It was a struggle hearing this news just before we were going to have a grand day, but I had to enjoy myself for Diana's sake.

I tell you this because my mom ended up moving to California with my aunt. It allowed a few more frequent trips for my mom to come visit. She tried to find herself and enjoy her freedom. We had offered for her to move in with us for a while and when she was ready, her and her dog came and lived with us.

It was so convenient to have a live-in babysitter. Tim and I would be able to go out on occasion just the two of us for a few date nights. My mom was also there to help Diana with her homework, go to her school functions, and show Diana how to hike and have a good time. Mom was here for about six months until she found a place in the mountains that was perfect for her. She ended up moving out but was only an hour and a half away. We are still able to see her on occasion, more often than if she still lived in Chicago.

Years later, when Diana was fourteen, my sister and her husband were getting divorced. My sister always wanted to move out to Arizona and now was her chance. She packed up herself and three of her kids (two stayed behind. One was in college, and another was going to finish high school where they lived). We offered for them to stay with us for a while to get back on their feet. We don't have a big house by any means, so it would be squishy in here. Three adults and four kids in a fifteen hundred square foot house. Diana was now going to experience what it would be like to have siblings and share her room and all her things with her cousins. She shared a room with two of her cousins, which meant the three of them were in her bedroom with not much room for anything else. In the loft would be my sister and one of the kids. We made it work for just shy of a year. The cousins would play together, fight together, just like a real family. It was good for her to have all this family together. When they moved out, they didn't move too far. They live just twenty minutes away and can still have sleepovers if they so choose.

Chapter Twelve

Diana made it through the year of school in first grade. She spent the majority of the year learning to communicate and speak English instead of understanding the basic academics. She struggled in school. Homework at night for a first grader would last hours and usually end up with her in tears. It was frustrating as I couldn't just make her learn and I tried so many different ways to see what would help her. If she finally understood something, by the next morning it was gone, she couldn't recall how to do it again.

Her teachers, along with Tim and I, decided we would hold her back yet again and put her in an English Language Learners (ELL) class. I did regret this decision, but I didn't know what to do. There was no way she would succeed in second grade, so we took a chance and put our now nine-year-old girl back in first grade. Diana actually looked like she belonged. She had a short stature and similar mentality, even though she was three years older than her peers. It was worth a shot to see if we could get her all caught up.

The issue with Diana now in an ELL class, was the rest of the students in the class spoke Spanish. While it's not allowed to be spoken in class, it still was. It was also spoken on the playground. Diana was an outsider. I even went to her class's parent teacher meeting, and they spoke Spanish the entire time. Every now and then, English was spoken because I was in the classroom.

This year was just as tough as the year before. She relearned everything she was taught the previous year yet didn't know it then and continued to not understand it. She had no friends. No one to play with. She was excited to be dropped off at school in the morning but would run to the other side of the fence and look through to wave good-bye to me. Off she would then go to play by herself. It was heart wrenching. She looked happy most of the time, but I wanted more for her.

I would become more and more frustrated with her school as they were supposed to test her and get an Individual Education Plan (IEP) in place. They kept stalling. Tim threw all his education training and knowledge at them and yet they still wouldn't budge. They would use excuses like she wasn't in school long enough or away from her native language long enough. We were beyond frustrated. It was clear she needed help. She was still in first grade and still couldn't grasp the idea of colors, numbers, and letters. After talking with Tim's coworkers, we decided when she went to second grade, we would be changing schools. We knew her current school had a lot of negatives, but once we experienced them, it was tough. Changing to a charter under the same district as her father, felt like the right move.

Her current school was so terrible, that the school nurse even called DCFS (Arizona Department of Children and Family Services) on us. Diana was at home eating breakfast and wouldn't keep all four legs of the chair on the ground, as most kids need reminders about. It happened that she fell backwards on the floor. She cried, but she was ok. Off to school she went, after receiving some hugs and kisses. She went to the school nurse later that day, I think for a band aid for a papercut, and that's when it unraveled. The school nurse didn't like us to begin with as we wouldn't come to pick up Diana for minor things like a headache, because she was sad, or even to bring a better lunch. She didn't like us because we wouldn't drop off new shoes that wouldn't have to be tied. She called us all the time. We realized Diana would go to the nurse's office often, because it would get her out of class from having to deal with not understanding the lessons inside the classroom. When Diana went to the school nurse this particular time, she obviously told her she fell out of the chair. The nurse was quick to call and claimed there were handprints on her back which would have represented a beating. When asking Diana leading questions, Diana would agree. She agrees with everything someone says because she doesn't understand the questions and she doesn't understand how to question another person.

That was one of the scariest days. I got the call from Tim that DCFS was going to have a meeting at our house with us and Diana that afternoon. I rushed home from work and joined Tim. We were so upset. We did everything to go through this adoption, why would we treat the child we tried for years to have that horribly. After meeting with the case worker, she quickly noticed we wouldn't have done anything like that and checked out Diana's back where the so called handprints would have been and she didn't even have any sort of marks anywhere on her body. Maybe a bruise on her knee from the playground. I completely understand that school nurses and administrators need to report anything suspicious they see, but to blanketly make up stories because you don't like us, went way too far. I was hesitant to even send her back to that school, but I didn't know where else to take her.

Before Diana's school year was up, we took her to a cardiologist as she clearly had heart surgery in her earlier years. It was the only thing we knew about in her medical history, and that was just because of her very large scar and uneven chest. We went to Phoenix Children's Hospital and were a bit concerned about what they would tell us and what they would find. It was a very good visit, however, from x-rays and MRI's, it was not clear what had been done in her previous surgery. Those same tests, however, revealed she would need another surgery on her heart. Her aortic valve was not functioning as it should, and it was causing her heart to beat so incredibly fast that you could literally see her pulse in her neck. It needed to be fixed. I was nervous as I never had any kind of surgery in the past, and now I had to send my daughter through yet another one. She didn't really seem to have too much memory of her last one except that the nurses were nice. We were told her surgery was in Russia, but we believe that to be a lie. The thing with the health history given by the orphanage is that most of it is just made up to sound good. They said they took her to the best hospital in Russia. Thinking about that years later, it just never made sense. If it was truly the best hospital in Russia, why would she even have such a deformed chest and her scar was so uneven?

We scheduled Diana's surgery towards the middle of May. Her school was frustrating me so much, I didn't even care that she would miss the last two weeks of school. It was going to be an eight-week recovery at home where she would have to lay low, so summer break just seemed like a perfect time for recovery.

The surgery was the longest seven and a half hours of my life. Waiting around the hospital, going to get lunch, waiting some more, and only had one update that things were going well. Finally, they were done. The nurse came out to us and let us know Diana would soon be back in her room and was getting ready to wake up.

I walked into her hospital room and just saw her attached to all sorts of wires. Her hair was all over the place. She was in her hospital gown looking helpless. I almost lost it as she appeared so healthy the day before. I knew I had to be strong for her. Diana woke up and was cranky and whiny. Something that's not typical of her. I couldn't imagine the pain she was in and how uncomfortable she must have been. She did make a great recovery in the hospital and only stayed for five nights before being released to come back home. At home she couldn't run or be very wild for the next few weeks as her breastbone was healing from being cracked open. I could no longer see her pulse through her neck, and her deformed chest looked a whole lot more normal. She made a full recovery, but unfortunately, she will continue to be on blood thinners her whole life because her replaced aortic valve is now a mechanical one. It's actually quite neat to hear her heartbeat as she ticks like a clock. The kicker of this whole thing is her pediatric surgeon, literally one of the best in the state, if not country, could not even figure out what was done in her past surgery. He guesses she had two previous surgeries, instead of one. He also guesses that maybe she had a hole in her heart that was patched up, but nothing indicates anything was really done. I just hope she didn't have surgeries where they just opened her up without fixing anything. Regardless, she is in good hands now and gets checked out semiannually by her favorite cardiologist.

With a summer recovery, Diana couldn't enjoy any swimming or running around. By the time the "be careful" time was up, she was a week away from starting her new school. It was a different experience for her as she would now have to wear a uniform to school. I for one am against uniforms but had to suck it up as I knew this was going to be a much better fit. As the school year went on, I continued to feel defeated. We had a first-year teacher, who wasn't sure how testing really worked or how to handle students with different needs. It was a tough year as well. She continued to get more homework that quickly became a nightmare. This school was much quicker to get an IEP in place for her and that did help a little. Unfortunately, she was still trying to learn her numbers and letters. Still trying to figure out how to read. She finally advanced to second grade but was not learning anything. In this classroom, students were more willing to help her out. We quickly realized, the kids who were helping her were really just doing the work for her and she didn't know how to do it. There was a major difference at this school, and it was the students. Most of the class wanted to be her friend. It didn't matter to them that she was older, or that she needed help. They knew she needed a friend and were there to be there for her. She didn't make any friends that she would hang out with during free time at home but did make friends to play with while in school. The other difference was the principal. She wanted to see things get better for Diana and she did everything in her power to move things along and get her the help she needed. It was a sense of relief. Someone that was on our side. Someone that believed in Diana and believed she could do it with proper assistance.

Diana was quickly happier in school and even had a crush on her second-grade teacher. Each day she fell behind more and more, but they were working with her now. I didn't feel as stressed, except when it came to homework. I remember one day in the beginning of this new school year; Diana came home expressing that she was now taking Spanish. I quickly called the principal, and we just had a good laugh. This child is still trying to learn English, she's clearly a slower learner, there's no way throwing another language in the mix was going to help anything. She was then able to help the principal with duties going forward rather than having to go to that class.

Third grade came and went. We had a teacher that we liked and was helping her. Students were all still interested in helping. Towards the middle of the year, her teacher decided that teaching was too much for her and was going to take a break. No!!! Finally, someone that we were able to work with was on our side, and she was leaving us halfway through the year. It was hard. There was a substitute the rest of the year, and we were at a loss. She must not have been too bad, because I don't remember her at all looking back.

Fourth grade started just like the other ones. The reminder to keep an eye on her food intake. Be patient with her in her studies. She made a really good friend at school who was a year older than her. He had Down Syndrome and they quickly became the best of friends. We were never able to connect with his parents unfortunately, so they were never able to hang out outside of school. A new principal took over. The one that supported us and understood our situation was now gone. It was very sad, but for the first time, I really felt like we were on the right track. Diana still continued to struggle and was nowhere near where her peers were in academics. She had a special education administrator working with her and we felt great. That was until we were completely blindsided a little before Christmas break. We were called into a meeting. They wanted us to send Diana to a different school that was over thirty-five minutes away from our home. At this school was a special needs class that she would be a part of for the rest of fourth grade through sixth grade. It was a lot of information to take in as we were not expecting it. I left that day feeling defeated. Feeling like no one wanted Diana in their class and just wanted to pass her off and be someone else's problem. It was a hard pill to swallow.

After much deliberation between myself and Tim, we decided to go on a school visit to see what this special classroom was all about. After meeting the teacher and listening to her talk about what they do in class, we decided to give it a try. I didn't want to keep bouncing Diana from school to school, but maybe we just didn't find the right school. We were going to have to find a new school for her at the end of sixth grade as it was, so maybe this wouldn't be so bad as this school is on the same campus as their high school. This new school was also a part of the same charter district. In her IEP they would write that she gets door to door transportation which meant the van or bus would come all the way to her and pick her up. There would be no more than fifteen kids in her class, and they would all get individualized learning. It sounded really good, but I was still unsure. I felt like we just got thrown out of her other school. I know it was in her best interest, and we could've denied their suggestion. We decided to give it a shot. Diana was excited to go to a new school in January. However, it was heart breaking when I picked her up from her school at Christmas break time. I've never seen her cry so much about missing her friends and teachers. I was just about to join her in those tears. We drove straight to her new school to sign some papers and she was all better and excited again about starting the new school.

Come January, she was officially no longer in a mainstream classroom and instead now in a special education classroom. It was such a great decision and I felt bad at how angry I got when it was first suggested to us. I thought mainstream was in her best interest originally. The teacher and aide in the classroom knew how to work with all sorts of needs and Diana quickly settled in. In her classroom were kids from kindergarten to sixth grade. She finally made really good friends with three boys. Kids that she actually had the opportunity to hang out with in social settings. Things were looking up.

Once seventh grade came along I got nervous again. She was going to the same school, but with a different teacher. This time her class would be seventh through twelfth grade. Seventh grade was a difficult transition for her as only one of her friends was moving on with her as her other friends were in lower grade levels. She had a teacher that was not very good. It seemed like all he ever did was put on movies for the students to watch. Sometimes they were educational; most of the time not. We often complained to her sixth-grade teacher, but there was only so much she could do. After a few months, we found out she made a really good friend who was in the other classroom. At this point I didn't know there was even another upper grade classroom. The teacher reached out to us, and we decided it was best for Diana to change classrooms. I couldn't imagine her stuck in this one for the next six years. Come eighth grade she moved classes and became best friends with this girl. They have now been best friends for years and I couldn't be happier she finally made a connection with someone.

While we feel she's finally on the right path and has lots of assistance at school, the bus situation was another story. One of the downsides of being on a special education bus is that other kids have different abilities and may not communicate in the same way. The driver is unable to keep an eye on everything going on and Diana has a very tough time with communication if something is wrong. We've had many incidents. Stealing of food, being stabbed by pencils, and the worst was an all-out sexual assault. I will not go into that to protect my daughter's privacy; however, the school told us about it months later and were not willing to do anything about it. We met with the police who advised that they couldn't find the kid because his family moved and didn't seem to care as well. That's where I learned that being a special needs mom is going to be so much more work than I had ever imagined. Protecting my daughter without being an overprotective mom would be my challenge.

Chapter Thirteen

I went on a tangent about her schooling, but how did we get to where we are now? Diana was diagnosed through her school, around second grade, with a mild intellectual disability. That's it. All her struggles and it was just considered to be mild. After doing a lot of research, I read on how many people that have unknown learning disabilities just consider them as mild and be done with it. It was good enough to get her IEP going, but not enough to really get appropriate help. There had to be something else. So many people say not to label kids, but I wanted a label. I wanted to understand her. I wanted to know how she could be taught something a million times, yet still doesn't know it. She couldn't do math, science, social studies, physical education, etc. without needing major assistance. She didn't understand how to follow more than one step directions. I was at a loss. I wanted to give her all the help in the world but didn't know where to start. I wasn't prepared for everything I would need to do.

With adoption from Ukraine, almost every child is labeled as having a disability. No one could tell us what kind of disability she had. It wouldn't have changed our minds on her, but I feel like I may have been able to help her earlier, had I had more information.

When Diana was about ten years old, her pediatrician suggested we try genetic testing. Doing the good ole Google searches brought us to many possibilities of diagnoses she may have. Tim and I decided genetic testing would be a good thing to try out. The doctor checked her hands, feet, facial features and swabbed her cheek. We went home after a long discussion with him. Weeks later the call I waited forever for came. The assistant told us nothing came up on her testing and that was it. I was relieved nothing serious came up, but we were back to square one.

We tried to apply for government insurance to help her receive the proper therapies she needed. We would go through many steps just to be denied as they felt mild intellectual disability wasn't that big of a deal. Without an actual diagnosis, we wouldn't be able to get her much needed speech therapy and occupational therapy unless we paid out of pocket. This would really add up and we wouldn't be able to afford it. I just finished paying off her hospital bill from heart surgery, so I wouldn't be able to add therapies on.

When Diana was in eighth grade, we decided to pursue different avenues. We again talked with her pediatrician who this time got us in touch with a behavioral psychologist. This was now during Covid time so only one parent was able to go in with her. All three of us drove to the hospital together. We chose Tim to go in with her and I would wait for hours in the parking garage or walk around on the outside of the hospital to pass time. I wanted her to know we were both there for her and for her not to be afraid. She was tested on everything, and the psychologist called me while Diana and Tim were in her office. She assured us everything went well, and she would go over all the tests and put together her report over the next few weeks. It was now just a waiting game.

In the meantime, we reapplied for Medicaid for her. Her Division of Developmental Disabilities (DDD) coordinator kept our hopes up letting us know almost everyone will be denied on the first try which is why we tried right away again.

We had our second interview with DDD and about a half hour later, we were to have our results from the psychologist. It was decided I would take the call with DDD and Tim would take the other call. Since it was Covid time, everything was still done over the phone. We were about to get rejected again as Diana was still listed as having a mild intellectual disability. Before I knew it, Tim came running to me. We at last had a diagnosis! Diana was officially diagnosed with Level Two Autism Spectrum Disorder and Moderate Intellectual Disability. I instantly told DDD about the new diagnosis and at last we were moving. Tim and I did not have a chance to process the information since we were concentrating on getting information from one person to another. We were ecstatic. All we truly wanted was a diagnosis which would open so many doors and opportunities for Diana.

We had to wait for paperwork to get processed, but as soon as Diana was diagnosed, everything moved quickly. Before we knew it Diana was being set up with speech and occupational therapies. One hour a week, she gets a speech therapist that comes to our home. Two hours a week Diana receives occupational therapy who also comes to our home. It was a huge achievement. If you or someone you know is also going through this process and is receiving denials, please remember to attempt to be patient and know that many people do get denied at first. Make sure everything is documented so they are unable to say no. It can feel like an uphill battle, but at some point, it will get better, and your child will have the help they need. For us, it really took us seven years since adoption. We didn't start looking into diagnoses right away. We assumed a lot of the equation was her moving to a brand-new country and not being pushed too hard while in Ukraine. It was apparent earlier on though that something wasn't quite right, and we were persistent until we got what we needed.

What exactly is Level Two Autism? Autism presents differently from person to person no matter where they are placed on the spectrum. Girls also present much differently than boys. This is the reason why girls are quite a bit harder to diagnose. According to Lane Regional Hospital, "In this level, individuals require substantial support and have problems that are more readily obvious to others. These issues may be trouble with verbal communication, having very restricted interests, and exhibiting frequent, repetitive behaviors."

In reality, it doesn't say much. For Diana, she continues to have speech issues. She can talk but not everyone can understand her. She has a hard time forming sentences. As mentioned before, she has a moderate learning disability. Her IQ is very low. At age eighteen and in high school, she continues to struggle with math. Not understanding adding or subtracting or money. She struggles with all subjects and can't recall what she was taught. When she comes home from school, she can't recall what she did that day and if she does remember, she can't come up with a speech to describe her day. This is a little funny though, because she can remember minor things from ten years ago that I wouldn't remember. She does a lot of rocking and hand gestures to ease herself if she is nervous. She has a hard time making friends and if she does, she can never remember their names. She wants to be included in activities but doesn't know how to talk to another peer unless they include her from the start. She gets hooked on different subjects. For a good five years straight at least, she was obsessed with red Dodge Ram's. For another three years she was obsessed with cement mixers. She used to be determined to be a Walmart truck driver when she was older. Now, she was obsessed with these things, but she didn't care to read and research about them. She would call out each one that she saw on the road. She was also obsessed with the movie Frozen, a bit beyond where most girls were.

Diana's reading is actually really strong at about an eighth-grade level. However, her reading comprehension is more of a first grader. Diana needs help with all projects we do, even if she's done similar things in the past. For example, selling Girl Scout cookies. We are going into her nineth year of selling, but every year she forgets the names of the cookies, how much they cost, how to make a sign, what cookies sell the best, etc. We always need to start fresh each year. As a mom, it's frustrating to go over everything over and over again, however more so it makes me sad. She works so hard and just can't remember things day to day or year to year.

Diana does not understand personal space or personal bubbles. She doesn't pick up on social queues. She will try to wear winter onesie pajamas in the middle of an Arizona summer because she can't understand or differentiate the difference of hot and cold. She will still mess up her opposite words because to her, it doesn't make a whole lot of difference.

As much as she would like to, driving is most likely not going to happen for her. Not only does she have a hard time learning the rules of the road, but she is unaware of her surroundings. She doesn't look where she is going and is constantly bumping into things.

Diana will most likely never live on her own. She will always need some sort of help. She may live with us forever or we may find a group home that she would feel comfortable with.

Her dad and I are always trying to help, but we try to get her to do what is being asked of her before we jump in. We strive to make her as independent as possible, and sometimes it takes a lot of work. I would love for her to attend college, find a career she loves, learn to drive, and move out one day to start her own life. I will never give up on her or those dreams, I am practical though in knowing those things may never happen, and that's okay. In the meantime, Tim and I have guardianship over her. We have made a legal document handing over our guardianship to a lifelong friend of mine if anything should ever happen to us. I will consider a group home for her one day, if it's extremely good. I will drive her around myself my whole life if I must. Regardless, she will be very well taken care of to live her happy life.

Six months before Diana's eighteenth birthday, Tim and I applied for guardianship over her. We didn't want to take any of her rights away, but for now, she is not independent enough to be her own legal adult. She has no way of income and is unable to make educational decisions regarding her health. In order to do this, we needed to head to the family courthouse and retrieve the blank packet of papers. We were able to take them home and fill everything out. There was an area for her pediatrician to fill out as well that would state she agreed with us for guardianship. The courthouse was nice enough to go over everything with us so we can ensure we fill everything out correctly. Once we filed and paid the fees, we waited for a court date. It took a few months before we obtained a date. We did explain to Diana from the beginning why we were doing this and to make sure she understood the best of her abilities.

It was finally time to head to court and we took Diana out of school so she could be there as well. We wanted her involved in the process. We arrived at the courthouse early and waited just outside the courtroom doors until a little before we would be called. We took a seat and watched other cases being heard. Finally, it was our turn. I was very intimidated. I keep my whistle clean and have never been in an American courtroom before. I watch a lot of crime shows, so that was all I had to reference. The judge seemed stern. However, once it was our turn, he lightened up, so I think it just may have been the tougher cases before ours. He talked to Diana a little and talked to Tim and I. Our entire case took no more than five minutes. He awarded us guardianship. Unfortunately, he took her driving privileges away during the guardianship and automatically took way her voting rights. This was hard for both Tim and I. We are, however, able to end the guardianship and any time if we feel we are ready to do so.

Conservatorship was another item we were contemplating. After much discussion and much research, we decided not to do this. The biggest reason was because she doesn't have any assets. There is really nothing but the tiniest of bank accounts to her name. Nothing major for us to manage. If she was willed a house or similar from someone, then we would want to go this route, but not for a typical family.

Chapter Fourteen

I don't want Diana treated differently because she has some special needs, however, I want her to be able to achieve success.

So how do we give Diana a normal life when it comes to activities? Well, we originally had her in cheerleading. It wasn't competitive or anything like that, basically just some tumbling. She was happy, but nowhere near where the other girls' abilities were. She managed to put on her performance and the next level would be competitive. We, as a family, decided to give something else a try.

Next up was a choir. I was in an adult choir, and she loved to sing. She may not be able to carry a tune, but she sure does have the heart. I found a performance choir that I thought she would enjoy. She got to wear a pretty dress and performed a few times. Unfortunately, this choir soon decided they were going to be competitive and there was no way she would be able to keep up, especially with not being able to read very well at the time. The music was tough for her.

Girl Scouts has become one of the best things for Diana. It teaches independence, working as a team, can be adapted if needed, and allows for some fun trips and a small group of girls at her grade level she would see once a week. It was perfect. I ended up being a troop leader as there was a need and I was previously a coleader for my neighbor. In Diana's second year of Girl Scouts, my mom was living with us at the time and agreed to be my coleader. She was a coleader in the past with my sister's troop back in the day.

We had a great troop, Troop 2100. I had a small group of girls in second and third grades. They were considered Brownies and we met weekly at my house. It was convenient not to have to travel anywhere. Diana absolutely loved it. Weekly we would do team building activities, like how to flip a blanket upside down while everyone was standing on it. We would do arts and crafts like making two hundred greeting cards for the children's hospital. We would sell cookies and Diana was always one of the highest sellers. We would go camping, hiking, shoot archery, and the list would go on. The biggest element would be teaching these girls to be good people. Every week they would bring some spare change to the meeting. At the end of the year, they were able to buy a whole bunch of things at the dollar store and would show acts of kindness to our neighbors. They gave supplies to make spaghetti dinner for a married couple, kid bandages for an urgent care, coloring books and stuffed animals to kids passing by. The biggest of them all, they purchased a meal at a nearby restaurant for the next person in line. That ended up creating a pay it forward that lasted a while. The girls were so excited.

It was a hard decision to leave the troop, but some of the girls moved on. Girl Scouts were still so important to us. I had decided we would try being Independent Girl Members (or IGM for short). This meant we would have no troop and it would just be the two of us working together. Home school for scouts. We were still able to do all the Girl Scout events, but I was able to really adapt to Diana's level. We did this for three years. Two years at a Junior level and one year as a Cadette. Diana was able to work hard and earn her Bronze and Silver awards by doing this. It was great quality time and we really enjoyed ourselves, but I could tell she was missing being with other scouts on a weekly basis. We made the decision to send her back to a troop.

This was great, I finally got a break from being a leader. We found a fantastic troop that has patience to work with her and encourage her to become a leader. There are all different ages of girls from kindergarten to those ready to graduate high school. This is where she is meant to finish out her Girl Scouting experience. She is working on earning her Gold Award with the help of her Occupational Therapist and plans to continue with scouts until she graduates high school.

We also wanted to get Diana into some sports. It was difficult for her as she was too old for beginners and too fragile (because of blood thinners), for competitive games. A suggestion from one of my friends was to investigate a Special Olympics program. It would be people with all sorts of abilities, and she would fit in perfectly. Upon looking into this, I found a fantastic adaptive program in Mesa. Mesa would be about a half hour drive, but they had so many options that we could try out.

Diana absolutely loved to swim. She was definitely a water baby but didn't really have the skills to do it. I took a chance and registered her for a swimming adaptive program. It was the best decision I made. She learned to be a great swimmer over the years. She learns how to compete, how to win with grace, how to lose with dignity, and how to be part of a team. Because this program was so great, we made the decision to allow her to try other sports. She has been in cheer, swim, theater, track (which was not her favorite), and multiple activities. Activities would include Bingo night, movies in the park night, and Christmas shopping. Once she turned sixteen she was able to take part in more activities, like dances. The adaptive program has been the only place that I really see Diana being herself. She has tons of friends and has such a great time. I suggest anyone looking into adaptive programs for those kids that would qualify. These programs I credit with having her grow the most. Not only is she able to stay in shape while doing sports, but she is also able to go forever if she wants. There is no age limit.

On a visit to Diana's cardiologist, they suggested that Diana attend a heart camp. It would be a camp filled with kids who also had heart conditions. They had volunteer nurses and a doctor on staff in case it was needed. It was a camp where all heart kids were given the opportunity to be themselves and not worry about other kids making fun of them because maybe they are slower, run out of breath quicker, or have a zipper scar. Diana was ready to go, but I was very hesitant. It would be the first time she was ever away from us for an entire work week. I was nervous because she would be just at the end of her recovery. I was nervous because a lot of people, especially when she was this young, had a hard time understanding her. After a lot of convincing and doing my research, I decided to let her go. They had phones up there if for any reason I needed to be contacted and she was only two hours away. I checked their social media sites often for any updates while she was gone. There were barely any pictures posted. Honestly, it was a good thing because it meant everyone was having so much fun. I finally came across a picture where I saw her in the background. Relief! My baby is growing up, going to camp by herself, and had a huge smile on her face. That was all I needed to see. The following weeks afterwards they finally posted all the pictures, and she was in a few. It looked like she really had the time of her life. In heart camp, they did zip lining, horseback riding, hiking, shooting guns (that freaked me out a little), archery, swimming, and had dance parties. Diana went to this heart camp all the way until she was seventeen, missing a few years because of Covid. When she was turning eighteen, she tried to volunteer to be a camp counselor. We waited forever for their response. Then it finally came. They denied her. It would be the first

116

time the reality of her being different as an adult would hit. She was devastated, but eventually was able to move on.

Another program we just found recently was a day program for adults with special needs. In this program they provide door to door transportation to and from their center, Monday through Friday. At the current moment, Diana is only able to go on school breaks, but once she graduates high school, she can go every day if she chooses. Typically, the program is for adults aged eighteen and older. They will allow age sixteen and older for those on school breaks. They get together and do activities together. Things like going to a nearby museum, playing educational games, cooking, watching movies, the list goes on. The purpose of this program is to teach these adults some skills so they can possibly get a job or live on their own one day.

The members are not meant to be there for the rest of their lives, while some may, the goal is to graduate them so they can become successful humans in society. Some may take years, but they go to better themselves daily.

Diana is in a class at school right now called Transitions. This class helps to prepare her for the real world. She may never live on her own, but maybe she will with assistance. This class is trying to show her what is out there. What she can do to make herself a better person and to contribute to society. They are looking into volunteer work she may be able to do. She has done a ton of volunteering through her years in Girl Scouts, but never anything without me or a leader nearby. This would allow her to experience having a boss and having a real job. I don't plan on having her volunteer forever, but to get experience under her belt and working with someone else besides mom, is really what she needs.

Another option through her school is a college prep program. I can't guarantee she will go to college, but there are classes she can take that will help her decide if it's something she wants to do in the future. Things like cosmetology or pastry chef are what is piquing her interest as of now.

Chapter Fifteen

Vacations are very important to our family. It is the time to go see family, friends, or even the world. We were fortunate enough to have several trips over the last ten years and even more fortunate to have people visit us. A few of them were mentioned before like going to Disneyland.

Diana's first trip to Chicago was for her cousin's eighth grade graduation. It was a great excuse for the three of us to fly out to Chicago and she could meet all the family and friends we still had there. She met aunts, uncles, a great aunt, cousins and was able to see her grandma and grandpa again. We would return to Chicago about two other times. Since then, most of our family has moved to other states, some to Arizona, so we stopped visiting there.

Diana soon became very close with our friend Kirsten. Kirsten was one of the people we were able to visit when we were in Chicago. I met her when I was in sixth grade, and she was the one that came with me to Philadelphia when I met Tim. She also made several visits to us almost yearly after Diana came home. She would stay with us for a long weekend and spoil Diana as much as possible. She would take her to the zoo, the Ostrich farm, shopping, etc. She would help her learn to tie her shoes and help with homework. Kirsten would come often until one day, she moved to Arizona! She lives around an hour from us, but now we can go to her house or she can come to ours anytime. Diana loves her visits.

We would have a couple trips to Philadelphia as well so she could see her Grandmom and uncles. She got to take a city tour, go to the Jersey shore in summer, see some museums and enjoy a Christmas celebration throughout her trips.

As a family, we would take a big trip to Colorado. We packed up the car and headed for a very long road trip. Diana would learn patience on this trip as it took several hours and several stops. I put together a snack bin for her that she absolutely loved. So many snacks were packed away just for her. We wanted to save money while on this trip so we packed all sorts of canned goods and easy desserts that we could make in the hotel room microwave. The hotel would have a free breakfast, which was really tasty, and we would pack sandwiches to go. We would then come back and have our canned goods, usually SpaghettiOs or soup, for dinner. We ate out maybe two times in total and saved a ton of money. While in Colorado we saw the Armed Forces Museum, attended a fall fest to pick our pumpkin, and visited where the Broncos play.

At Christmas time one year, Santa gifted Diana a huge box. Inside that box were tons of blown-up balloons. In the middle of the box was a Harry Potter cloak along with a brown paper bag that held a piece of paper. It was an invitation for Diana to visit Universal Studios for the first time. She was so excited, and Santa managed to pull off the surprise. That January we drove out to California and stayed at a little dumpy motel just a couple minutes from the park. We stayed at the park from open to close the next day, not missing a thing. We were able to go on every ride, some more than once.

Another one of our super memorable vacations was going to Montana, Idaho, and Wyoming. We flew this time and rented a car. We drove down to Idaho and visited the potato museum and saw many potato fields. We drove back up to Montana and visited Yellowstone. Yellowstone was where the majority of our trip would be. It was so beautiful. We saw bald eagles, deer, and bison. We saw so many hot springs while we were there too.

Our most recent vacation was a two-week cruise to Hawaii. This was planned for quite some time. We drove our own car to Los Angeles and parked in the cruise car park, boarded the cruise and off we went. Tim and I were on a cruise in the past, but this was Diana's first. We spent five days at sea where Diana was able to learn how to hula, play ukelele, eat however much she wanted, whenever she wanted, and could even play in the casino. Our first stop was in Kona on the big island. There we went snorkeling, bought myself and new ukelele, and we took a farm tour and learned about how they make spices and chocolate. In Honolulu, Uncle Joe decided to meet us there. He drove us around and we went to see Pearl Harbor. We also visited a beach to swim and ate some shave ice. While in Kauai we took a UTV adventure ride. I let Diana sit up front in the side by side and we all got incredibly filthy. In fact, after several washes, the clothes we wore there are still not clean. It was raining on and off throughout the day and saw so many beautiful rainbows. We were supposed to visit Maui, but unfortunately about two months before we were to go, was the great fire that destroyed the island. We still plan to visit one day. The cruise ship took us to Hilo on the big island instead. Tim really wanted to visit the seahorse farm, so that's how we spent our day. We had another five days at sea, followed by a stop in Ensenada, Mexico. Diana was old enough to have her first (and probably last) margarita. She was not a fan.

We already have two other cruises planned and she is so excited to go. We live simple lives so we can make these trips happen. These trips aren't just great for our family to spend quality time together, but they really help with Diana's education. She is a hands-on learner and going on these trips really makes her understand the places we travel. She also has great opportunities to practice speaking with others and learning proper etiquette while in public settings. I hope we will always be able to travel. It helps her grow so much.

When we are not planning a vacation we try to do some fun activities. There is honestly not a lot to do in the Phoenix area unless it involves hiking or camping. Diana and I will go camping a lot, but it's a very specific time that we can go. It is way too hot to camp in the summer and way too cold to camp in the winter. The best places to camp are up north in the mountains. The problem with that is we tent camp, and it's freezing all winter. We did go camping once in the valley, and it was quite boring. We minus well just camped in our backyard. Nothing but desert all around us. Up north there's beautiful trees and you can feel so at peace.

One of our best camping experiences was at Roosevelt Lake. We had a spot right next to the water. Diana and I love to kayak, and we brought both of ours with us. We just had them sitting at the end of our site, we would play Uno (her favorite game), get in the kayak for an hour, come back, make lunch, and back out we went. When we weren't on the water or playing games we would take a nap in the hammock. We have a tradition when we go camping. Diana has a fuzzy snowball that lights up when it's hit. We will play toss while in the camp after it's pitch-black outside. There are always lot of giggles as she's a professional with hitting me in the head. The camping trips are always so relaxing, and we both come back feeling rejuvenated.

The one and only time Diana and I were able to convince Tim to go camping with us was when we were headed to Sea World. Tim managed to get free tickets since he was a teacher and we wanted to keep the trip cheap. The nice thing about living in Arizona is we can drive to a lot of the California theme parks rather than fly. We went pretty easy on Tim. We didn't pick a spot that was totally secluded, we made our meals using the small propane stove, and didn't do any rugged camping activities. We were only at our campsite to sleep and eat. We went to Sea World the last year where Shamu was allowed to perform. It was a fantastic day seeing the whales and the dolphins, petting the sting rays, and just walking around enjoying each other's company.

Diana has been to a total of three concerts, and she just loves them. Her very first concert was by Bon Jovi. To save money on parking we would park where I used to work and take the light rail the rest of the way in. The light rail is like a train, except it stops at all stop lights and usually doesn't take us near anywhere we want to go. In this case, it did take us just a block from the stadium. Diana was so excited to attend and stood the entire concert while screaming and singing. Bon Jovi is my favorite band, so I was excited to share the experience with her.

Another year at Christmas time, I gave Diana, Katy Perry tickets. Just me and her would go. It was perfect because Carly Rae Jepsen was the opening act. "So Call Me, Maybe" was the first English song Diana ever knew and would sing to us while we were still in Ukraine. Diana couldn't wait to go to this concert as this was truly for her. She was the one that liked both singers. We got up to the stadium nice and early and had time to eat dinner while there. We stopped at the candy shop and bought all sorts of goodies that were able to come in with us and off we went to the show! When I was booking the tickets, I wanted the best seats I could find. I found two aisle seats, in two different rows, but right next to each other. I had Diana sit in front of me and we were still able to talk. There was a large man in front of her and the couple sitting directly next to her offered to move her over a couple seats so she could see better. It was amazing watching her reaction as Katy Perry performed songs that she knew. All in all, I've been to several concerts in my lifetime and this one was one of the best.

Speaking of concerts, Tim and I always enjoyed going to see Trans Siberian Orchestra as Christmas is approaching. The three of us headed out, Diana in a very pretty black and silver dress, and headed for the concert. We did not tell Diana what the concert was about or what music they would be playing. We wanted it to be a surprise for her. She enjoyed their first hour of story time and recognized some of the songs. If you've ever been to a TSO concert, you know that after story time is a huge rock concert. Diana couldn't believe her eyes. The fire, the strobes, the loud rock music. She had never seen anything like it before. It was worth keeping it under wraps to really see her reactions.

The circus is always a childhood favorite of mine, and I was excited one year to be able to take my own child. This was the last year they were going to use elephants in the show, and I wanted Diana to be able to see. When we arrived, we made it early enough to join the pre circus party on the stadium floor. She was able to dance with clowns and see if she was able to juggle. Afterwards we took our seats, bought some cotton candy, and enjoyed the show.

Around the same time Disney's Frozen on Ice was happening. We of course had to see that. Diana was obsessed with Frozen, especially with Elsa. What kid wasn't, right? Diana held onto this obsession for years and even now it's still one of her favorites. She loved being able to see Elsa ice skating around the rink.

We have been to many basketball games, football games, hockey games, etc. But there was one hockey game in particular that really stands out. It was Girl Scout night, meaning Girl Scouts were able to get discounted tickets. Diana met the Phoenix Coyote mascot, Howler, and was ready for the big game. Why was it so special this time? Diana got to ride the Zamboni! A few days before we went to the game, Tim decided to write the Coyote's a letter about Diana. We didn't think we would ever hear a response from them, we were just wanting to let them know how excited Diana was about going to a game, if anything we thought maybe they would give us a coupon for a free hot dog. We were shocked when she invited Diana to ride the Zamboni in between the second and third period. I was so happy for her, I had tears of joy. I took so many pictures and videos of her sitting on it waving to the whole crowd. Tim, well, he was very jealous as he always wanted to sit on one.

One of our favorite pastimes is kayaking. Well, Diana outgrew her kayak and decided she rather paddleboard. We have a nice lake out here and try to go often. Believe it or not, we try to avoid going in the summer. It's just too darn hot out there and there are crowds everywhere. We like the slower seasons, when you can really enjoy the beauty of the desert all around you. My favorite thing to do is lay back in my kayak and look at the mountains all around covered with cacti. Every single time, it just amazes me that this is where we live. Coming from Illinois, all we had were flat roads, corn fields, and the occasional hill. There was one time we were kayaking in the winter (wet suit pants are highly suggested) and we saw the mountains in the distance. They were covered in snow. Here we were on a gorgeous not so cold day, staring at the snow on the mountains. Again, truly beautiful.

Some people may think we spoil Diana with all these things, but the truth is, we are careful where we do spend our money. To us, experiences are way more important than stuff. She doesn't play with the latest toy craze, and we don't buy her many electronics. Anyone can do experiences; the memories will last a life time.

Chapter Sixteen

One thing I always wish I could do was to home school Diana. I just know that I could teach her more than what she learns in school. Three reasons that I don't. Diana needs to socialize. Yes, she's in activities, but she doesn't socialize all that much more than two people. Secondly, I have a full-time job and it would be very hard for her to stay home all day doing nothing and then do schooling at night. This wouldn't work either as it would interfere with her activities. Diana needs someone to be hands on or close by to help her with her work. Both Tim and I now work at home, however, we would be working and not necessarily have the time to stop everything to help her with a question. The last reason is patience. I don't have as much patience as I would like to have. I tend to get frustrated if I explain something twenty times and she still does not understand. This is in no way her fault; it just gets very hard for me. Therefore, school is really the best place for her to be.

That being said, I needed a way to help her with a lot of life skills that she either learned once and forgets, or skills that used to be taught in school and no longer are.

I came up with a binder for Diana. Each skill I would write out. Things like learning parent's phone numbers, her own address, or how to address an envelope. We would go over these skills and write down the date she learned them. She would then go back to it maybe a couple days or a couple weeks after the fact. She may not remember, or she may remember. We would then write the practice date and a summary of what she learned. We would wait another couple days, weeks, or months depending on the skill and see if she truly mastered. Master would be where she knew, say the address, and could tell me where she lived without any additional help. If she did, we would write the mastery date down. If she didn't, we would write down another practice date and do it again until she had it mastered. Even once mastered, we would still go back and see if she still remembered. Mastering something still takes practice.

After talking to her Occupational Therapist and others about what we were doing, they all tried to convince me to make a book. It was something I never really thought about, but it seemed like a lot of people were urging me to do it.

I was recalling one of my psychic sessions where she told me that one day I would make a children's book. I laughed at her as I didn't see that ever happening. I thought about it a few times in the past, but never really knew how to go about it or how to get it started. I decided, maybe I really should turn my activity into a book.

That is how my first book, "Learning to Live: Life Skills for ALL Ages" was born. It all started with me trying to help Diana. I have had a good amount of success in the short time it has been released. I've had so many people look through my book and just comment how much they appreciate it being written and excited to help their children, whether special needs or neurotypical, use the book. I even sold over thirty-five books to the adult day program so they could make their curriculum based off the book.

I encourage Diana and every kid or young adult to work through the book in their free time. It's not like they would need to spend hours with their faces in it. Take an activity or two at a time and learn, practice, then master.

Who would've thought I would have published a book and now I'm on my second. I do love writing. My plans are to write a typical children's book and will hope to do that in the near future. Diana is such an inspiration to me. She fights every day to get through the day and I can honestly say, I don't think I would be able to handle the things that she handles day in and day out.

Chapter Seventeen

Where does the future take us? Nobody really knows. I always want to see Diana happy, after all, who wouldn't want to see their kid happy. I touched on a few things in prior chapters but will talk about them in more detail here.

Diana is now a legal adult, and it scares me. Even though I have legal guardianship, she is still responsible for getting through this thing called life. I can do everything I possibly can to protect her, but that bubble wrap will never be enough. People are rough out there. People are mean. When she was a kid, her disabilities were more accepted. Now that she's an adult, they are not. It sounds bad to say, but it is the truth. People look at her differently now that she is older. They feel she should know more than she does. They don't know how to act with someone with different abilities unless they are a small kid. It is something I know I will never get used to. I'm relieved that Diana doesn't notice.

Diana will constantly need Speech and Occupational Therapy. When she goes a couple weeks without Speech, whether in school or at home, it's very noticeable. She will start to slur her words and begin to mumble making it even harder to understand her. Occupational Therapy has been great to work with hand eye coordination, following directions, and more. If we were to stop either one of those therapies, she would start to go backwards.

Diana is trying to get some volunteer work under her belt. Again, now that she is an adult, it is much harder for her to obtain. When she was a kid it was more understandable if she didn't understand the directions. Her transitions teacher is working with her but haven't found anyone to accept her working for free. They are told right off the bat about her situation and yet, no one responds. If she does get a volunteer call, that would be great, but I want more for her. It is much harder for adults with special needs to obtain paying jobs. Most of the time they are told to volunteer somewhere. They are missing the point that these adults want to contribute to society. They don't want to always work for free. I have seen grocery stores open their hearts and hire those with intellectual disabilities, which has been fantastic. Hopefully one day more will follow. There's always a job that can be done in any business by those with intellectual disabilities, unfortunately many don't want to take the time to train and retrain these individuals.

When out shopping I have noticed Diana will get dirty looks from employees if she asks them a question or if she answers a question they ask. Granted, usually when Diana answers a question, it actually has nothing to do with what was being asked. However, when she was a kid, employees would just laugh it off. Now, she will get awkward stares.

I don't want to say college will never happen for her. However, I'm realistic. Diana needs so much help at school now that I couldn't imagine her doing college type work. There are more colleges and universities opening their doors to those with special needs, so that maybe in the future we will find a good fit. There are trade schools, but the trade schools will still have a similar layout of work. But, for now, we aren't discussing college as a family.

Her aunt is working hard on helping Diana with learning how to decorate cakes. Maybe one day a bakery will take a chance with her, or she can run her own business with my help.

Group homes are not as voodoo as they once were. There are a lot of group homes these days. If we decide to go that route, it would be way in the future. As of now, I enjoy having Diana at home, after all, she is still in high school. One day I'm sure she will want more independence. The group homes are great. They take their members to the grocery store or their activities. They check in on them to make sure they are taking care of household chores like dishes and sweeping. They make sure they are showering and taking care of themselves. It is definitely an option in the future, but it still scares me as of now.

Sometimes I wish she was "normal". I mean really, what is normal. In society it is accepted a lot more to be normal without needing extra assistance. I want her to have a normal high school life where she hangs out with friends at the mall and restaurants without parents around. Where she goes on dates. Where she can pass a test. Part of acceptance as a parent is accepting that your child is not going to necessarily do those things. They might do some and they might not. It's okay. They are just living a different life than you had envisioned. If Diana was considered "normal", what would that be? For one, it wouldn't be her. She is happy, she gets excited about everything, she has a best friend who she can hang out with at the house every now and then. Nobody is normal. Being accepted for who you are is everything.

She has been left out of Girl Scouts as she can't relate to the older ones and can't relate to the younger ones. She has been left out of typical high school activities like sports or dances. I don't expect her to be always included, I was never always included in things in my younger years either.

We are looking towards how she has been accepted. She has been accepted with the other kids and adults in her adaptive programs. Most Girl Scouts accept her for who she is. Her best friend accepts her for who she is, as does her family.

I don't prance around asking everyone for awareness. Let's face it, everyone, or at least most people, are aware of Autism and learning disabilities. I'm looking more for acceptance. Everyone is different. I'm different than you; you're different than your friend. But, we all need to accept those with different abilities that we are not used to. I've met countless kids and adults with disabilities of all sorts, and the only thing they truly want is to be able to fit in.

Tracy M. Dayment is a wife, mom, and cheerleader for her daughter. Originally from Chicago, then transplanted to Arizona, she writes about her own experiences with adoption and having an autistic child with intellectual disabilities. Having a child with differences has opened her eyes to a different type of world.

For more books by Tracy M, Jackson, visit
www.daymentlegacybooks.com

DAYMENT
LEGACY BOOKS